Using Data Analysis to Improve Student Learning

Toward 100% Proficiency

Ovid K. Wong and Ming-Long Lam

D1607595

ROWMAN & LITTLEFIELD EDUCATION
Lanham • New York • Toronto • Plymouth, UK

Published in the United States of America
by Rowman & Littlefield Education
A Division of Rowman & Littlefield Publishers, Inc.
A wholly owned subsidary of The Rowman & Littlefield Publishing Group,
Inc.
4501 Forbes Boulevard, Suite 200, Lanham, Maryland 20706
www.rowmaneducation.com

Estover Road
Plymouth PL6 7PY
United Kingdom

British Library Cataloguing in Publication Information Available

Library of Congress Cataloging-in-Publication Data

Wong, Ovid K.
    Using data analysis to improve student learning : toward 100%
proficiency /
    Ovid K. Wong and Ming-Long Lam.
        p. cm.
    Includes bibliographical references
    ISBN-13: 978-1-57886-479-9 (cloth : alk. paper)
    ISBN-10: 1-57886-479-8 (cloth : alk. paper)
    ISBN-13: 978-1-57886-480-5 (pbk. : alk. paper)
    ISBN-10: 1-57886-480-1 (pbk. : alk. paper)
    1. Education—Data processing.   2. School improvement
programs—Data   processing.   3. Academic achievement—Data
processing.   I. Lam, Ming-Long, 1962–   II. Title.
    LB1028.43.W556   2006
    379.1'580285—dc22   2006017762

We acknowledge the higher-order inspiration of the book and the support of our wives, Ada Wong and Gina Lam.

Contents

List of Figures

Foreword

Today, probably more than at any other time in the history of public education, we face an age of accountability. Schools are required to submit to the mandates of federal and state authorities to provide information regarding the competence of their students. Whether it be test scores on reading and mathematics measures given on a regularly scheduled basis, or through some other means, public schools must comply with these requirements in order to support their continued funding and in order to meet stipulations for annual yearly progress.

Many view these requirements negatively, citing justified concerns related to the learning and teaching environment, the supposed increase in teaching to the test, the additional paperwork necessitated by such requirements, the lack of flexibility in the curriculum, the pressure that such requirements place on students, and a myriad of other issues. Others view these requirements positively by utilizing these requirements as an opportunity to tell their stories. These schools have been successful in demonstrating to all concerned the prowess of their curricula, the needs being met by their schools, the quality of their teachers and other educational staff, the use of student data in the improvement of school functioning, as well as any number of other points of success that they can identify.

The present text attempts to assist schools, administrators, and teachers to make use of the current requirements for accountability. The authors—Dr. Ovid Wong, a veteran award-winning educator in curriculum, instruction, and assessment, and Dr. Ming-Long Lam, with a strong background in statistical research—provide the reader with historical information that has led to today's requirements for accountability and the use of data for student improvement, a useful discussion of student data for improvement and accountability, an indication of professional practice and its relation to school program data, a plan for moving the data collected to the district level along with implications of this move, and a vital link to utilizing all of this information in the development of continuous school improvement plans.

Taken as a positive step forward, this text will provide the reader with a sound basis for using today's accountability requirements as a framework for school improvement. Half of improving the instruction in schools is knowing what needs to be done. This goal is achieved by developing a strong system of data collection, analysis, and interpretation. Then the task is to take what we know and develop plans for the improvement of instruction. I extend my compliments to the authors for leading the way in making this transition from data to school improvement, and in writing a text that is both useful and accessible.

Steven C. Russell, Ph.D.
Dean, College of Education, Governors State University,
University Park, IL
November 2005

Introduction

The purpose of the book is to help readers use data effectively toward 100 percent student and school proficiency. What are data, and why are they important? Data are facts, simple and pure. Without data support, any statements, claims, or decisions for improvement will just be the opinion of yet another person. This book shows you what important data to collect and how they are analyzed, interpreted, and communicated for accountability.

How will schools respond to the use of data to improve students? Schools with different levels of resource support will handle the task differently. Schools in a large system will have the department of research and testing take on the task. Schools with less resource support may have the technology coordinator or the school principal perform the task. Schools with limited resources may just train teachers to tackle the job. Regardless of who has the job and the resource options, the effective use of data for improvement is not an option when we are serious about student success.

This book begins with where we were more than two decades ago in education reform and the ever-pressing need to improve students. Chapter 2 presents data tasks that classroom teachers deal with typically and routinely, including the analysis of attendance, test scores, and the development of data-driven strategies. Chapter 3 delves into more data tasks at the school level, including student academic performance disaggregated into learning standards and student demographics. Other studies review the relationship that opportunity to learn and instructional style have to student achievement. Chapter 4 broadly views school studies dealing with the assessment of school culture and school effectiveness. Finally, Chapter 5 puts the data together strategically in the continuous school improvement plan as a tool for action and communication. For every case study discussed in the book we offer you a step-by-step process to analyze the data with suggestions for improvement. We assume that the reader has some basic knowledge in using Microsoft Excel to allow more focus on the content of the discussion. In addition, we will be describing the advanced features of data analysis and interpretations.

1

Paving the Road to Using More Data for Student Improvement

What is the purpose of education? This question has stimulated and puzzled people for ages. One common answer is the acquisition of knowledge and skills. Another view is that the purpose of education is to give students the curiosity to explore and a desire to learn. Even more comprehensive is the statement that the true purpose of education is to develop successful lifelong learners.

In time, American education has gone down an extended path to attain the desirable outcomes of producing successful learners. Two decades ago the quality of American education was described in *A Nation at Risk*. The report defined the problems afflicting American education. Seven years later, the Goals 2000: Educate America Act was established. It set goals by providing a national reform framework to improve student achievement. More recently, the No Child Left Behind Act made it a law that all students and schools are accountable for new levels of accountability. One thing is apparent when we look at the shaping of American education through time. There is an increasing demand for defining purposeful goals and reaching higher levels of academic success for all students.

A NATION AT RISK

The National Commission on Excellence in Education published a landmark federal report entitled *A Nation at Risk* in April 1983. This

1

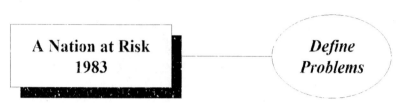

A Nation at Risk
1983

Define
Problems

report, under the administration of President Ronald Regan, claimed
that American education programs are less than rigorous. The schools
suffered from loose standards and many teachers were not well prepared. This report also cautioned that the flawed educational system
would cause the weakening of the nation's economy, social structure,
and defenses. The beginning of the report sets the tenor of risks in
American education.

> Our Nation is at risk. Our once unchallenged preeminence in com-
> merce, industry, science, and technological innovation is being over-
> taken by competitors throughout the world. This report is concerned
> with only one of the many causes and dimensions of the problem, but
> it is the one that under girds American prosperity, security, and civility.
> We report to the American people that while we can take justifiable pride
> in what our schools and colleges have historically accomplished and
> contributed to the United States and the well-being of its people, the
> educational foundations of our society are presently being eroded by a
> rising tide of mediocrity that threatens our very future as a Nation and a
> people. What was unimaginable a generation ago has begun to occur—
> others are matching and surpassing our educational attainments.

A Nation at Risk was a wake-up call for public education improvement. It is interesting to note that of the thirteen risk indicators mentioned in the report, 62 percent are related to student achievement.
This focus of student achievement set the stage for an elevated level
of accountability through student assessment. The general recommendations from the report such as effective leadership, public commitment, and other educational processes were presented but offered
limited resource support.

What are the responses to *A Nation at Risk*? First and foremost, education has become a permanent issue on the national agenda. Many
states have established academic standards and instituted new testing
programs to measure achievement toward standards. Some states

have enacted comprehensive education reform legislation. The legislation raised graduation requirements, decreased the average class size, required students to pass standardized tests, redesigned teacher-licensing requirements, and more. In essence, *A Nation at Risk* was a key catalyst for a nationwide education reform.

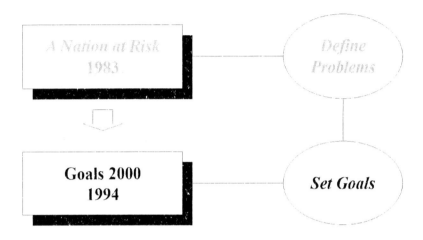

AMERICA GOALS 2000

On March 26, 1994, during the Clinton administration, the Goals 2000: Educate America Act was passed by the U.S. Congress. It was intended to improve schools by providing national goals to ensure fair educational opportunities and high student achievement. The goals are organized into eight categories: (1) school readiness, (2) school completion, (3) student achievement and citizenship, (4) teacher education and professional development, (5) mathematics and science, (6) adult literacy and lifelong learning, (7) safe, disciplined, and drug-free schools, and (8) school and home partnership. Goals 2000 declares that by the year 2000:

- All children will start school ready to learn.
- The high school graduation rate will increase to 90 percent.
- All students will leave grades 4, 8, and 12 with competency in English, mathematics, science, foreign languages, civics and gov-

ernment, economics, arts, history, and geography. Every school in America will ensure that all students learn to use their minds well to prepare them for responsible and productive citizenship.

- The teaching force will have access to professional development opportunities to acquire the knowledge and skills needed to prepare all students for the next century.
- American students will be first in the world in mathematics and science achievement.
- Every adult American will be literate and prepared to compete in a global economy and exercise the rights and responsibilities of citizenship.
- Every school will offer a disciplined environment conducive to learning with no drugs, violence, or unauthorized presence of firearms and alcohol.
- Every school will promote partnerships with parents to increase the social, emotional, and academic growth of children.

Goals 2000 supports state efforts to develop rigorous standards to guide what every student should know and be able to do. The improvement efforts were focused on improving student achievement according to standards.

What are the responses to Goals 2000? The focus on standards prompted accountability changes in curriculum, instruction, professional development, assessment, school and leadership organization, parental and community involvement. What is accountability? The term implies a systematic method to ensure the improvement of schools. Accountability is improved education and achievement, not ranking, sorting, humiliation, or headlines. The key question of accountability is not, Which student is better? but Do our students meet or exceed the standards? and What teaching and leadership strategies can we use to have more students achieving at high levels? The elements of accountability are goals, success indicators, data analysis, and reporting procedures with rewards or sanctions. The demand to provide accountability led to the development and implementation of the state assessment systems. Under Goals 2000, state assessment systems are aligned to state standards to include, with few exceptions, the testing of all students.

Unfortunately, national guidelines for the inclusion of testing of all students were inconsistent. Many elements of standard implementation for assessing special needs students, for example, were not addressed or developed. Last but not least, there was no clear accountability to sustain the improvement efforts.

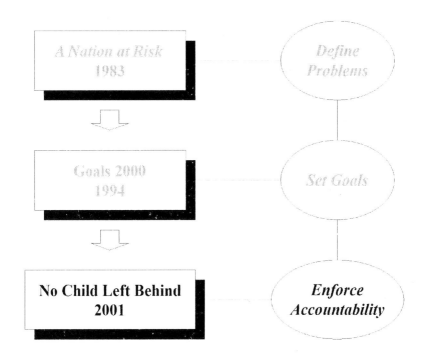

NO CHILD LEFT BEHIND

The No Child Left Behind (NCLB) Act of 2001 has been prominent in the education arena. Prior to NCLB, the measures of success have not been focused heavily on academic achievement. With NCLB school success is measured mainly by whether or not children learn.

How do schools across the nation answer to the NCLB mandates? All schools must develop and implement schoolwide accountability systems. These systems will:

- Set academic standards in each content area to show what students should know and be able to do.
- Collect data through tests aligned with the academic standards.

- Use test data to identify strengths and weaknesses in the system.
- Report school condition and progress to parents and communities.
- Empower parents to take action based on school information.
- Celebrate schools that make progress.
- Direct changes in schools that need help. Some examples are public school choice, supplemental student services like tutoring, after school help, and summer school.

Parents and citizens equipped with academic results can now make informed decisions about education. NCLB requires that school information be released in states, school districts, and schools through annual report cards on the following:

- Student academic achievement disaggregated by student subgroups
- Comparison of students at basic, proficient, and advanced levels of academic achievement
- Attendance and graduation rates
- Professional qualifications of teachers
- Percentages of students not tested and school status if identified for school improvement

How do schools/districts determine the success of NCLB? The answer is by the measurement of adequate yearly progress (AYP) as directed by the federal law. AYP measures (1) student participation rate in the state assessment system, (2) academic performance, and (3) graduation rate. AYP further requires the disaggregation of test data in reading and mathematics by different student subgroups. The subgroups are white, Native American, Asian, Hispanic, black, English-language learners, economically disadvantaged, and students with disabilities. A comparison of the Wisconsin AYP model (Figure 1.1) and the Illinois AYP model (Figure 1.2) shows that the level of math and reading proficiencies are different. Despite the state differences, all students need to achieve 100-percent proficiency by the year 2014. This final destination of reaching the 100-percent proficiency target speaks for all students across the nation. Figure 1.3 describes the AYP criteria and how schools attain AYP status.

If a school or district does not make the performance target, it can still make AYP if there is a 10-percent decrease in student scoring non-proficient from the previous year. This process is called safe harbor. If

AYP (Adequate Yearly Progress) Requirements

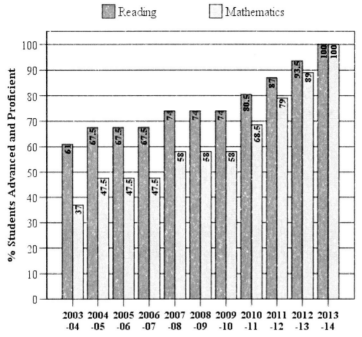

Figure 1.1.   The Wisconsin AYP Model

a school receives Title I funds and does not make AYP for two consecutive years, the school is placed on school improvement. If the school does not make AYP for a third year, it must provide supplemental educational services for low-performing students. Finally, if the school continues to fail AYP, it progresses into corrective action and then restructuring plans.

USING DATA FOR IMPROVEMENT

In the past decades we have witnessed the rigorous shaping of American education. Reflection shows that each era of education reform has escalated accountability in more testing aimed at higher student achievement and more effective schools.

8   *Chapter 1*

AYP (Adequate Yearly Progress) Requirements

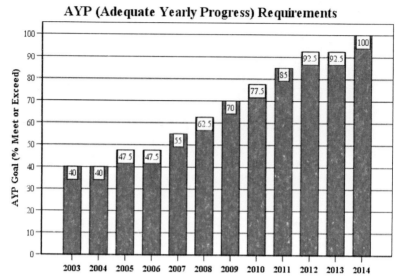

Figure 1.2. The Illinois AYP Model

Who is responsible for student achievement and school improvement? In a typical educational system a division of labor model shows five levels of organization. They are classroom, department or team, building (the school), grade level (across the district), and district. Realistically, all the stakeholders in the system will not want to get involved equally in every effort for improvement. Hence we should make the assumption about which responsibility people will deem important. Teachers should generally be responsible for student achievement in their classrooms. School principals should generally be responsible for coordinating student achievement in their schools. District office staff and administrators should generally be responsible and articulating student achievement in the grade levels. In the following chapters different student improvement tasks will be described in respective of the different-level stakeholders of the school organization starting from the classroom.

What data can we collect to reach high student achievement and effective schools? Figure 1.4 shows that there are three main data sources: student data, professional practice data, and school community perception data.

Data available to the educators are massive. If they are not carefully

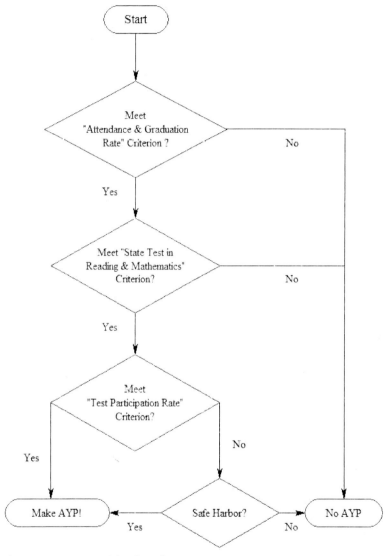

Figure 1.3.   How Do Schools Make AYP?

Note: AYP = adequate yearly progress.

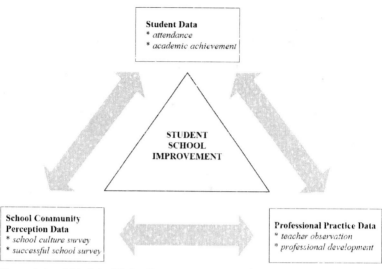

Figure 1.4.   A Model of Using Data to Improve Students and Schools

managed for analysis the end result can be perplexing and inconclu-
sive. Let us look at the massiveness of school data. Educators collect
and manage common student data as they go about doing their business of educating. Teachers may carry with them a student record
book that contains student attendance and other classroom data.
Another important student data source is the state and local assessment information. Under the NCLB law we now have to manage the
student demographic data that describe the uniqueness of each student such as English-proficiency status, special needs, or racial/ethnic
status. The school report card also shows student enrollment and student state test participation data. The data depict where each student
spends his or her time in class, extracurricular activities, and other stu-
dent-supporting services. Visit the school's office and look into a student cumulative folder. The folder will enlighten the reader about the
complexity of school record keeping.

What strategies would you use to work with the student achievement data? Do you use attendance records and behavior referrals to
show what each student values through his or her actions and attitudes? Do you use course enrollment data in athletics, music, drama,
and clubs to describe where each student spends his or her time in the

school? Do you review the cumulative data by subject area performance? If you are a high school teacher, do you study the national examination data such as ACT or SAT referencing the scores with the student course of preparation? Do you compare the composite score to the individual subscores to identify the strengths and weaknesses? We raised a number of data questions just to amplify your acuteness toward the many facets of student data.

What are the data sources for professional practice? One of them is the staff certification data indicating the subjects the teachers are certified to teach. Under the NCLB law the public can now request the professional qualifications of the teacher. How about professional development data? They inform us the types of training in which the staff participate in continued education. Professional practice data are extremely important for improvement simply because high-quality teaching begets high-quality student learning.

What are the data sources for school community perception? Parent involvement data tell us about the involvement of parents in the school. Parent perception data also tell us about the satisfaction of parents in the school. Interestingly, referendums passed can be a reflection of community satisfaction in the school. Have you seen opinion survey reports in your school? This is definitely a good source of perception data.

In addition to understanding the three main data sources we also need to assess data availability. Data must be made available to the school improvement team in the quest for 100-percent proficiency in students and schools. Find out if the data are available in electronic or paper form and who has access to the data and start the collection and sorting. After this broad data sources overview we are now ready to work with simple student data in the next chapter.

CHAPTER REFLECTION

1. What are the key findings of the *A Nation at Risk* report?
2. How did school systems respond to the *A Nation at Risk* report?
3. Compare the successes and failures of schools under the *A Nation at Risk*. Please illustrate with examples.
4. What are the main initiatives of Goals 2000 and how do the nation's school respond to the goal proposal?

5. Compare and contrast the plans for school improvement contained in *A Nation at Risk* and Goals 2000.
6. What is the main thrust of the No Child Left Behind law that is different from *A Nation at Risk* and Goals 2000?
7. "The No Child Left Behind law is unrealistic for classroom practitioners." Evaluate the credibility of the statement and support your response.
8. You are hired as a consultant to improve schools. What are the initial steps that you might take to assess the schools?
9. Develop a plan to coordinate the use of different data sources to improve a school with low student achievement.
10. Give an example of using student data and professional practice data jointly to improve a school not meeting the adequate yearly progress.

REFERENCE

United States National Commission on Excellence in Education. 1983. *A Nation at Risk: The Imperative for Education Reform: A Report to the Nation and the Secretary of Education.* Washington, D.C.: United States Department of Education.

2

Student Data, Improvement, and Accountability: Setting the Stage for Success

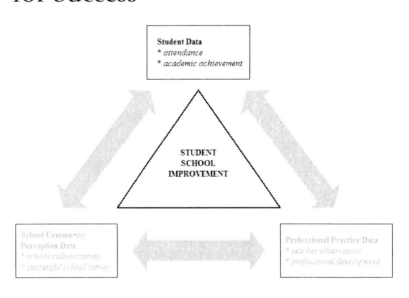

Student attendance and student learning are the basics of every school day. In this chapter we will learn to collect and analyze student attendance and learning data. Let us visit a fourth-grade class and learn how the attendance and learning data are processed and used to improve students.

The morning bell at Washington Elementary School rings at 8:45 A.M. The teacher is at the classroom door with a warm smile welcoming the fourth-grade students to a new school day. Students chatter to one another, shuffle through their backpacks for homework, and quickly settle into their seats. The students begin working on the bell ringer activity written large and clear on the chalkboard. Seeing that the students are engaged with the morning activity, the teacher quietly logs on to the electronic student record spreadsheet on the computer to check the class attendance.

STUDENT ATTENDANCE: SETTING THE STAGE FOR SUCCESS

The teacher is meticulous about keeping accurate attendance records for two reasons. The first one is related to students' opportunity to learn: the teacher strongly believes that the extent of students' opportunity to learn bears decisively on student learning. Teachers can only teach if students come to school. The second reason is critical to the school system: the third Friday student count in September and the second Friday count in January determine the flow of state revenue to the school.

Let us view the teacher's electronic record book (Figure 2.1) and see how attendance data are entered and processed with the help of Excel. The student attendance record has four essential features: (1) the attendance code located on the top left corner, (2) the vertical columns to include students' names (the first column) and the dates, (3) the horizontal rows representing the individual student attendance records, and (4) the three daily attendance summary rows at the bottom (Figure 2.2). To enter the attendance data, the teacher uses the appropriate codes such as T for tardy, P for present, UA for unexcused absence, and EA for excused absence.

To keep accurate student attendance, the teacher needs to (1) rename the spreadsheet, (2) enter the attendance data, and (3) calculate the data summary.

Rename the spreadsheet: The Excel spreadsheet file is, by default, named **Sheet1**, **Sheet2**, and so on. The sheet names are displayed as tabs in the lower left corner of the Excel window. The teacher renames the spreadsheet for identification purposes. Use the following four steps to rename a spreadsheet:

1. Move the cursor to the default name, say **Sheet1**.
2. Click the right button on the mouse.

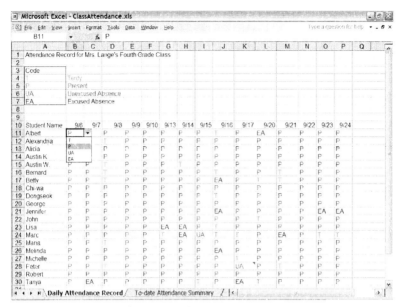

Figure 2.1.   Daily Attendance Record 1

3. Select **Rename** from the pop-up menu.
4. Enter the desired name.

In this example, the teacher named **Sheet1** as Daily Attendance Record and **Sheet2** as To-date Attendance Summary.

Enter the attendance data. It is okay to enter data manually by typing the value into a cell one at a time. Nevertheless, the teacher will find data entry less time-consuming when he or she can select from a prepared value list. Use the following three steps to prepare a value list:

1. Select the **Data** menu on the top, then the **List** submenu, and finally the **Create List** item.
2. Enter the cell range of the attendance codes ($A$4:$A$7 in this example; the $ sign indicates the absolute cell range in Excel) when an Excel dialog appears.
3. Hit **OK.**

The teacher uses a prepared value list to enter attendance code. Use the following four steps to prepare a list for the 9/6 column:

Microsoft Excel - ClassAttendance.xls

File Edit View Insert Format Tools Data Window Help   Type a question for help

B32   =COUNTIF(B11:B30,"=P")+COUNTIF(B11:B30,"=T")

	A	B	C	D	E	F	G	H	I	J	K	L	M	N	O	P
4	T	Tardy														
5	P	Present														
6	UA	Unexcused Absence														
7	EA	Excused Absence														
8																
9																
10	Student Name	9/6	9/7	9/8	9/9	9/10	9/13	9/14	9/15	9/16	9/17	9/20	9/21	9/22	9/23	9/24
11	Albert	P	P	P	P	P	P	P	P	T	P	EA	P	P	P	P
12	Alexandria	P	P	T	P	P	P	P	P	P	P	P	P	P	P	P
13	Alica	P	P	P	P	P	P	P	P	P	P	P	P	P	P	P
14	Austin K.	P	P	P	P	P	P	P	P	P	P	P	P	P	P	P
15	Austin W.	P	P	T	P	P	P	T	P	P	P	P	P	P	P	P
16	Bernard	P	P	T	P	P	P	P	P	T	P	P	T	P	P	P
17	Betty	P	P	T	P	P	P	P	P	EA	P	T	T	P	P	P
18	Clewa	P	P	P	P	P	P	P	P	P	P	P	P	P	P	P
19	Dongseok	P	P	P	P	P	P	P	P	T	P	P	P	P	P	P
20	George	P	P	P	P	P	P	P	P	P	P	P	P	P	P	P
21	Jennifer	P	P	P	P	P	P	P	P	EA	P	P	P	P	EA	EA
22	John	P	P	P	P	P	P	P	P	P	P	T	P	P	P	P
23	Lisa	P	P	P	P	EA	EA	P	P	T	P	P	P	P	F	P
24	Marc	P	P	P	P	P	T	EA	UA	T	T	P	EA	P	T	T
25	Mara	P	P	T	P	P	P	P	P	P	P	P	P	P	P	P
26	Nleinda	P	P	P	P	P	P	P	P	EA	P	P	P	P	P	P
27	Michelle	P	P	P	P	P	P	P	P	P	P	P	P	P	P	P
28	Peter	P	P	T	P	P	P	P	P	P	UA	P	T	P	P	P
29	Robert	P	P	P	P	P	P	P	P	P	P	P	P	P	P	P
30	Tanya	P	EA	P	P	P	P	P	T	P	EA	T	P	P	P	P
31																
32	Attendance	20	19	20	20	20	19	18	19	17	18	19	19	20	19	19
33	UA	0	0	0	0	0	0	0	1	0	1	0	0	0	0	0
34	EA	0	1	0	0	0	1	2	0	3	1	0	1	0	1	1
35																

Daily Attendance Record / To-date Attendance Summary /

Figure 2.2. Daily Attendance Record 2

1. Use the mouse to highlight the cells of the column (B11:B30).
2. Select the **Data** menu, then the **Validation** item.
3. When an Excel dialog comes up, select **List** from the **Allow** pull-down menu and enter the range where the attendance codes are defined ($A$7:$A$7 in this example) into **Source** field.
4. Hit **OK**.

Now the teacher is ready to use the prepared value list to enter the attendance code for the first student, Albert. Use the following four steps to enter Albert's attendance code:

1. Move the cursor to Albert's cell for 9/6 and click the left button on the mouse.
2. A drop-down menu with an arrow indicator now appears to the right side of the cell.
3. Click the arrow indicator and a menu appears.
4. Select and click the correct code (P in this example for Albert).

The teacher repeats the above steps and enters the attendance codes for the rest of the class.

Calculate the data summary. The teacher summarizes the attendance of the class. To do that, the teacher creates three summary rows just below the student attendance record. The first row is the number of students present (including tardy), the second row is the number of unexcused absence students, and the last row is the number of excused absence students (Figure 2.2).

The teacher calculates attendance summaries using the COUNTIF worksheet function in Excel. This function counts the number of cells within a range that meets a given criterion. The function takes two parts. The first part is the range of cells from which to count. For example, the summary range for 9/6 is B11:B30. The second part is the criterion in the form of an expression in which the cells will be counted. For example, to count the number of students present, the criteria are "= P" and "= T" to represent student present and student tardy respectively. Use the following four steps to calculate the number of students present on 9/6:

1. Click on the Daily Attendance Record tab (in the lower left corner).
2. Move the cursor to the correct cell (B32 in this example).
3. Type the formula: = COUNTIF(B11:B30," = P") + COUNTIF (B11:B30," = T") in the formula bar above the sheet. Please note that the total number present includes the number tardy.
4. Hit **Return.**

The summary value will then appear in the cell B32 representing the total number of students present on September 6 (9/6). The record shows that the teacher has perfect student attendance on that day. Similarly, the teacher calculates the number of unexcused absences on 9/6 using the formula: = COUNTIF(B11:B30," = UA") and the number of excused absences on 9/6 using the formula: = COUNTIF(B11:B30," = EA").

Although the teacher can repeat the process used for entering codes for 9/6, he or she can, however, use a shortcut for the next day, 9/7, without repeating the previous data entry steps. The shortcut steps are:

1. Use the mouse to highlight the entire column for 9/6 (B10 to B34).
2. Select the **Edit** menu, then the **Copy** item (the cells B10 to B34 are now enclosed by flashing dash lines).

3. Use the mouse to highlight the next column for 9/7 (C10 to C34).
4. Select the **Edit** menu, then the **Paste** item.

Now the 9/7 column mirrors the 9/6 column. The teacher then makes small adjustments to customize the 9/7 column:

1. Change the date from 9/6 to 9/7.
2. Change the appropriate attendance codes for the students.

The teacher notices that the three summary rows for the 9/7 column are updated automatically.

The teacher has twenty students and the attendance record shows a fifteen-day record from September 6 to September 24. What can one say about the class attendance based on the record? From the record, one can vertically eye scan the individual date column. One can identify the twenty students and their individual attendance with reference to present, tardy, and excused and unexcused absence. A student record sheet is easy to view when the data pool is small, with only twenty students and fifteen days. However, when the information is compiled or rolled up to a quarter, a semester, or the entire school year with 108 days, visual inspection of data will not be possible. For that reason, a To-date Attendance Summary is developed (Figure 2.3) to simplify the attendance date interpretation.

The teacher wants to summarize the to-date attendance record for each student and starts a new worksheet in the same Excel file. After renaming the worksheet from **Sheet2** to To-date Attendance Summary and adding the titles, and so on, he is ready to add the student names. Instead of entering the names into this new worksheet one at a time, he links the names from the Daily Attendance Record sheet to this newly created sheet. How does the teacher create the link? By adding a prefix to a cell in a worksheet, he can link the cell from one worksheet to a cell in another worksheet. The prefix is the quoted name of the referenced sheet and the exclamation mark (!). Use the following four steps to link the two worksheets:

1. Choose a cell (A12 in this example) to start.
2. Type in the formula bar: = 'Daily Attendance Record'!A11.
3. Hit **OK**.
4. Copy this cell (A12) to other cells (A13 to A30).

Microsoft Excel - ClassAttendance.xls

File   Edit   View   Insert   Format   Tools   Data   Window   Help

B12   =COUNTIF('Daily Attendance Record'!11:11,"=P")+COUNTIF('Daily Attendance Record'!11:11,"=T")

Attendance Record for Mrs. Lange's Fourth Grade Class

Code	
T	Tardy
P	Present
UA	Unexcused Absence
EA	Excused Absence

Most Recent School Day   9/24

Student Name	Present	Tardy	Unexcused Absence	Excused Absence	School Days	% Tardy	% Unexcused Absence
Albert	14	1	0	1	15	6.7%	0.0%
Alexandra	15	1	0	0	15	6.7%	0.0%
Alicia	15	0	0	0	15	0.0%	0.0%
Austin K.	15	0	0	0	15	0.0%	0.0%
Austin W.	15	2	0	0	15	13.3%	0.0%
Bernard	15	3	0	0	15	20.0%	0.0%
Betty	14	3	0	1	15	20.0%	0.0%
Chi-wa	15	0	0	0	15	0.0%	0.0%
Dongseok	15	1	0	0	15	6.7%	0.0%
George	15	0	0	0	15	0.0%	0.0%
Jennifer	12	0	0	3	15	0.0%	0.0%
John	15	1	0	0	15	6.7%	0.0%
Lisa	13	1	0	2	15	6.7%	0.0%
Marc	12	5	1	2	15	33.3%	6.7%
Maria	15	1	0	0	15	6.7%	0.0%
Melinda	14	0	0	1	15	0.0%	0.0%
Michele	15	1	0	0	15	6.7%	0.0%
Peter	14	2	1	0	15	13.3%	6.7%
Robert	15	0	0	0	15	0.0%	0.0%
Tanya	13	2	0	2	15	13.3%	0.0%

Daily Attendance Record   To-date Attendance Summary

Figure 2.3.   To-date Attendance Summary

Now all the student names show in the new worksheet.

The teacher wants to know four pieces of student attendance data to date: (1) the number of days present (including tardy) in the class, (2) the number of days tardy, (3) the number of unexcused absences, and (4) the number of excused absences. The teacher again uses the COUNTIF worksheet function. Since the teacher wants the to-date numbers, he leaves out the column names (e.g., B) in cell ranges. For example, to count all cells in row 11 of the Daily Attendance Record sheet, he specifies 11:11. Use the following three steps to calculate the number of days present for Albert:

1. Move the cursor to the correct cell (B12 in this example).
2. Type the formula: =COUNTIF('Daily Attendance Record'! 11:11,"=P") +COUNTIF('Daily Attendance Record'!11:11,"=T") in the formula bar above the sheet.
3. Hit **Return**.

The result of 14 will then appear in the cell B12.

By following similar steps, the teacher uses the formula: =COUNTIF ('Daily Attendance Record'!11:11, "=T") to calculate the number of tardies; the formula: = COUNTIF('Daily Attendance Record'!11:11, "= UA") to calculate the number of unexcused absences; and the formula: = COUNTIF('Daily Attendance Record'!11:11, "= EA") to calculate the number of excused absences for Albert. The results are put into cells C12, D12, and E12 respectively.

Besides the numbers, the teacher wants to know the percentages of tardy and unexcused absence days against the total number of school days. First, he creates a column named School Day (column F) that is the sum of numbers of days present, tardies, unexcused absences, and excused absences. In this case, the number of school days should be the same for all students. The teacher uses the formula = B12 + D12 + E12 for Albert. The sum value is put into the cell F12. Next he calculates the percentage of tardy days for Albert using the following five steps:

1. Create a column for the percentage (column G in this example).
2. Use the formula = C12/F12. The result is put into the cell G12.
3. Select the **Format** menu, the **Cells** item, the **Number** tab, and the **Percentage** from the **Category** list.
4. Choose the desired number of **Decimal Places** (one in this example).
5. Hit **OK.**

The value in the cell G12 is now formatted as a percentage. Similarly, the teacher calculates the percentage of unexcused absences for Albert in cell H12. Finally the teacher copies the cells B12:H12 (for Albert) and pastes them to the rest of the class. What we have seen thus far might appear to be a lot of effort to prepare a student attendance record. Is it worth the effort? You bet! Once the worksheet template is laid, taking student attendance for the rest of the school year will be as easy as the click of a mouse.

Based on the two worksheets, what appropriate student attendance questions may one ask? Who is likely to come to school and who is at risk of not coming to school? The attendance worksheets can answer these questions adequately because the answer is based on the attendance record. The rate of unexcused absences for Marc (6.7 percent) and Peter (6.7 percent) is noted based on the first fifteen school days. In addition, Marc and Peter have a record of coming to school late. Statisticians make projections based on an established data record. The teacher thinking like a statistician may want to make a hypothesis that Marc and Peter are likely not coming regularly to school. However, this prediction may change if the teacher continues the attendance record into the school year and implements intervention strategies.

A teacher will ask questions about the causes of student attendance problems. Unfortunately, the worksheet data fall short of giving the answer. The record thus far has helped us identify which possible students are problematic in school attendance. This is an important first step to determine the cause and solutions to address the problem.

FACTORS AFFECTING STUDENT ATTENDANCE

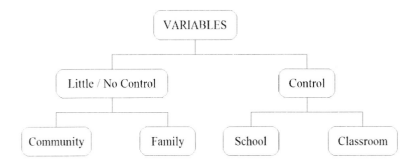

Equipped with attendance data, educators can begin their search for solutions to address the problem. What does a student attendance problem tell us? It is an alert that the student is disengaging from the school process. It may reflect a lack of student motivation and/or weak parental support. Variables affecting school attendance can be related to the community, family, school, and classroom (i.e., teacher or student). What are variables? Things that we measure, control, or manipulate in a study or research. To understand the big picture of poor student attendance we need to distinguish variables over which we have little control and variables on which we can have an impact to change. It is only natural that we want to invest more time and resources investment into the variables that we believe will make a difference.

Community variables that contribute to poor school attendance are intricate because they deal with the structure and the culture of a complex organization. This is especially true in an inner-city community where the problems may be a lack of school community support compounded by a high incidence of criminal activities. Family-related variables to poor attendance could be low family income, high family mobility, dysfunctional home life, non-English-speaking home, and low parental expectations. Research has shown that family income or the socioeconomic status (SES) of a family is a strong predictor of student success. For example, the federal Title I program uses the calculation of the low SES students for funding appropriation. The mother's level of education is another good predictor of student success . Interestingly, in an interview with the twelve *American Idol* finalists, seven pointed out their parents, especially their mother, as their idols. Family involvement may be education's best-kept secret. Of all the elements in the education process, positive parental involvement is very effective. We will discuss this topic in more depth when we present the school improvement research in Chapter 5. The community and family variables affecting school attendance are, however, variables over which we have little or no control.

What variables can we impact to alleviate student attendance problems? They are the school and student variables. School variables are related to school governance, for example, school governance and its enforcement, the school climate, curriculum, instruction, and counseling. School variables also include teachers and staff working collaboratively to support students. Student variables are essentially students' attitudes and behaviors. Low self-esteem, problematic peer relationships, drug abuse, pregnancy, truancy, and academic failure are manifestations of students' attitude and behavior problems.

PREVENTION AND INTERVENTION STRATEGIES

Truancy is unexcused as well as excessive absences. In some big cities unexcused absences can number in the thousands each day. Truancy is one of the top major problems in this country's schools, negatively affecting the success of our students.

How can schools help? There are a number of strategies that a school can use to combat truancy. The cardinal reference guiding these strategies is the firm establishment and implementation of an attendance policy based on the compulsory school attendance law. It is important that school staff respond to an attendance problem

according to the black-and-white policy in lieu of making decisions according to one's personal disposition. Are you familiar with the local attendance policy? Do you feel confident in responding to a problem following the policy? Educators who have input in defining the attendance policy should ensure that the policy is clear, well publicized, enforced, and flexible enough to deal with extenuating circumstances.

Low achievement, retention in grade, and behavioral difficulties are highly predictive of students dropping out of school. Consult with school services personnel to determine if the student might have a specific problem interfering with learning. Assessment of possible learning and behavior problems might help identify appropriate services to help the student to be more successful. Schools can systematically track student attendance, test scores, grades, behavior referrals, school attitudes, and family participation in school records. These records can provide information to identify students most at risk for being truant and thus refer them for appropriate prevention efforts. Prevention efforts might include incentives and supports to improve attendance, programs to encourage parent involvement, early intervention for academic difficulties (such as peer tutoring programs), community and school-based mentorships, and partnerships with community business to connect school to work. Development of high school alternative programs that provide nontraditional approaches to vocational training and high school completion will also provide options for students who have not been successful in meeting the academic requirements of the regular school program.

How can teachers help? In addition to schoolwide strategies and programs, school staff can be the role model and the enabler for students. Instead of focusing on why the student is unsuccessful in school, have the student identify goals that he wants to achieve from the school experience. Have him or her share school, home, and personal barriers that prevent him from reaching that goal. Sometimes talking about getting past the barriers to reaching the goal helps focus the efforts more productively than just complaining. Or quitting. Teachers can encourage the student to attend school regularly and to get involved in at least one extracurricular activity such as clubs or athletics programs. These activities make the student feel part of the school community and more motivated to perform in order to participate. If a students' lack of academic success restricts them from every activity, they often will see no value in continuing to try. If they are unable to meet these needs in the school setting, they often will find ways to meet these needs in less desirable ways.

One strategy that a teacher can use to prevent attendance problems is to give students the desire to come to school by giving them a taste of school success. Students tend to repeat the same behavior (coming to school) to achieve the same successful experience. Teachers need to assess their own behaviors and ask the following questions to see if they are helping students to be successful:

- Is my classroom management behavior fair and consistent?
- Is my class environment conducive to learning?
- Is my teaching clear, relevant, and engaging?
- Am I helping the students to develop and achieve academic goals?
- Am I addressing learning problems and providing appropriate intervention?
- Am I helping students develop good study habits?
- Do I build students' self-confidence by appropriate student recognition?
- Do I focus on my students' learning, always assessing the effectiveness of my own teaching?

Working toward 100-percent student and school proficiency begins with good school attendance. This is why the No Child Left Behind (NCLB) law requires schools to attain a high percentage of school attendance. As educators we need to set a high priority for school attendance thus paving the road to student success.

ANATOMY OF STUDENT ACHIEVEMENT DATA

There are many types of student achievement data filed in a school system. The data inform the subject tested, the grade level perform-

ance, the student subgroup performance, individual student performance, and more. To improve students, the data need to be dissected and interpreted with appropriate recommendations.

For many years, achievement data examine an aggregated or whole student group. Aggregated student data has the distinct disadvantage of masking the most important information: the information about individuals. For example, one can make an overarching comment like, "The seventh-grade science performance from Lincoln School is in need of improvement." Such a generalized statement addressing the whole seventh-grade student group is practically useless. It offers no real substance to suggest improvement. Let us rephrase the comment and say, "The seventh-grade English Language Learner (ELL) students from Lincoln School are in need of science improvement." This comment is a little more usable because it includes the subject and what specific student subgroup to focus on. From the second comment one can even drill down further to pinpoint the tested area. Let us revise the comment one more time to say, "The seventh-grade students enrolled in the Lincoln School English Language Learner (ELL) program are in need of improving Science Learning Standard 13." What we have done is separate or disaggregate the data into discrete information categories.

We can disaggregate student achievement data in two ways. The first way is student data disaggregation and the second way is content area disaggregation. The last comment is a combination of both student and content area disaggregated data.

To illustrate the disaggregation of the content area, the following chart shows the anatomy of the three Illinois science learning standards and their respective performance indicators by grade levels. One can see that the Science Standard 13 mentioned previously is much more than an identification number. It is a specific Illinois science learning standard that deals with the concepts of science, technology, and society.

Illinois Science Learning Standards	Standard General Description
Standard 11	*Understand the processes of scientific inquiry and technological design to investigate questions, conduct experiments, and solve problems.*
Standard 12	*Understand the fundamental concepts, principles, and interconnections of the life, physical, and earth/space sciences.*
Standard 13	*Understand the relationships among science, technology, and society in historical and contemporary contexts.*

Performance Indicators by Grade Levels:

EARLY ELEMENTARY	LATE ELEMENTARY	MIDDLE/JUNIOR HIGH SCHOOL	EARLY HIGH SCHOOL	LATE HIGH SCHOOL
13.A.1a Use basic safety practices (e.g. not tasting materials without permission, "stop/drop/roll").	13.A.2a Demonstrate ways to avoid injury when conducting science activities (e.g. wearing goggles, fire extinguisher use).	13.A.3a Identify and reduce potential hazards in science activities (e.g. ventilation, handling chemicals)	13.A.4a Estimate and suggest ways to reduce the degree of risk involved in science activities.	13.A.5a Design procedures and policies to eliminate or reduce risk in potentiallly hazardous science activities.

The subset of the chart shows that Science Standard 13 at the seventh-grade level (look under middle/junior high school in the chart)

is further categorized as 13.A.3a with the performance indicator of
"identify and reduce potential hazards in science activities." A rule of
thumb for helping a student to improve is to collect and analyze data
that are specific to the learner.

Study the following science assessment two-year report. In the
report student achievement is divided into four categories: minimal
performance, basic, proficient, and advanced with reference to what
students know and are able to do according to the science learning
standards. In this example, how do the report data support the claim
that Learning Standard 13 is in greatest need of improvement in
2004? Can you rank order the learning standards in priority of
improvement? What is the data trend over time?

Seventh-Grade Science Assessment, a Two-Year Report

Illinois Science Learning Standard	Minimal Performance	Basic	Proficient	Advanced
2004				
Standard 11	10%	40%	25%	25%
Standard 12	10%	35%	30%	25%
Standard 13	5%	65%	20%	10%
2005				
Standard 11	10%	30%	30%	30%
Standard 12	10%	30%	35%	25%
Standard 13	5%	60%	20%	12%

Based on the chart, Standard 13 is most need of improvement in
2004 because it has the lowest percentage of proficient and advanced
students. In 2004, Standard 13 has 30-percent proficient and
advanced, Standard 11 has 50 percent, and Standard 12 has 55 percent. From 2004 to 2005, Standard 11 moved from 50-percent to 60-
percent and Standard 12 moved from 55-percent to 60-percent proficient and advanced. Unfortunately, Standard 13 increased only from
30-percent to 32-percent proficient and advanced. Over time, Standard 11 made the most gain in student achievement (i.e., 10 percent).
Although Standard 12 in two years attained the same level of proficient and advanced, the gain (i.e., 5 percent) is less than Standard 12.
Finally, over time, Standard 13 made only a 2-percent gain. Data
trend over time is perceived as more reliable than data from an isolated or single occurrence incident.

The principal of Alton Elementary School reviews the Wisconsin
state report card about his school. It includes three components:
(1) all-student, all-subject data, (2) special education student reading
data, and (3) economically disadvantaged student reading data.

Chart A iş an all-student report showing grade 4 student achievement in reading, language, mathematics, science, and social studies. There are four student performance levels: advanced, proficient, basic, and minimal. Can you rank order the subject in priority of improvement using Chart A? Does Alton school meet the 2005 Wisconsin adequate yearly progress (AYP) in student achievement as prescribed by the NCLB law? How do you find out?

Chart A

Subject	Enrolled	WSAS	Min Perf	Basic	Proficient	Advanced
Reading	55	0%	18%	24%	45%	13%
Language	55	0%	14%	25%	49%	11%
Mathematics	55	0%	47%	13%	40%	0%
Science	55	0%	9%	49%	38%	4%
Social Studies	55	4%	10%	22%	35%	29%

Note: WSAS = Wisconsin Student Assessment System

Chart A shows the achievement data of five subjects. The percentage of proficient and advanced students from high to low ranking order is social studies (64 percent), language (60 percent), reading (58 percent), science (42 percent), and mathematics (40 percent). The school achieved a 58-percent proficient and advanced in reading (AYP requires 67.5 percent) and 40 percent in mathematics (AYP requires 47.5 percent). For that reason Alton does not meet the 2005 AYP student achievement requirement. Consult Figure 1.1: the Wisconsin AYP Model for the specific percentage of reading and mathematics requirements.

Chart B is a grade 4 special education student reading data report. What is the achievement difference in the combined percentage of proficient and advanced between students with disabilities and students without disabilities? How do you reference the chart data? Is Alton Elementary meeting the 2005 requirements of the NCLB mandate based on Chart B? Please explain.

Chart B

Student Type	Enrolled	No WSAS	Min Perf	Basic	Proficient	Advanced
Students with Disabilities	11	0%	72%	18%	1%	9%
Students without Disabilities	44	0%	5%	25%	57%	14%

The achievement difference between students with disabilities (10-percent proficient and advanced) and students without disabilities (71-percent proficient and advanced) is 61 percent (71 percent − 10 percent = 61 percent). Alton Elementary does not meet the 2005 AYP requirement of 67.5-percent proficient and advanced in reading. Again, consult Figure 1.1: The Wisconsin AYP model for the specific percentage of reading requirement.

Chart C is a report of economically disadvantaged students showing grade 4 achievement in reading. What is the achievement difference between the combined percentage of proficient and advanced between students who are economically disadvantaged and students who are not? Based only on the data from Chart A, Chart B, and Chart C is Alton Elementary meeting the requirements of the NCLB law? Please justify your answer.

			Chart C			
		No	Min			
Student Type	Enrolled	WSAS	Perf	Basic	Proficient	Advanced
Economically	46	0%	18%	26%	41%	15%
Disadvantaged						
Not Economically	9	0%	22%	11%	67%	0%
Disadvantaged						

The achievement difference between the combined percentage of proficient and advanced between students who are economically disadvantaged and students who are not is 11 percent (67 percent − 56 percent = 11 percent). Alton Elementary School does not meet the 2005 AYP requirement in reading and mathematics (Chart A), special education students (Chart B), and economically disadvantaged students (Chart C). We need to keep in mind that to satisfy the AYP requirement, a school has to meet the standard in student achievement in reading and mathematics, state test participation, graduation, or attendance.

Student achievement data come literally in bundles. If the data are not unbundled methodically to extract the information, we may get caught being data rich but information poor. Aggregated data define the big picture of information. Disaggregated data, on the other hand, define a specific area that makes up the big picture. In the example presented in Charts A, B, C, the principal of Alton Elementary has seen some disaggregated information about student achievement. He needs to do more investigation to better understand the specific standards that students struggle and develop plans for improvement.

STUDENT ACHIEVEMENT I: A SIMPLE
MEASURE OF SUCCESS

In this section we will examine student data in one class and then combine two classes to examine student data in a grade level. Finally we will analyze the achievement of a disaggregated student group.

A teacher is prepared to teach geometry following the school district's curriculum. To ensure the effectiveness of her instructional design she first assesses the readiness of the students. She then uses the student readiness (i.e., prior knowledge) data to design and drive the instruction. Prior knowledge is the first component of K-W-L. The teacher applies the K-W-L strategy developed originally by Donna Ogle of the National-Louis University. In this strategy model the *K* stands for the prior knowledge of the learner or what the student already knows. The *W* stands for what the learner wants to learn or find out. Finally, the *L* stands for what the learner learned. The K-W-L strategy helps teachers connect existing prior knowledge to new information then provide further opportunities for extended learning. The teacher uses the K-W-L chart throughout the study unit to connect student learning to adjust her teaching.

K-W-L CHART

What the student knows (*prior knowledge*)	What the student wants to find out (*goal setting*)	What the student learned (*accountability*)
---------------------------	-------------------------------	---------------------------

To find out the students' prior knowledge the teacher administers a brief geometry pretest to her students dealing with the properties of shapes. She assesses the prior knowledge of her students thus activating the K component of the K-W-L strategy. The teacher scores the test carefully and enters the data in Excel for analysis and interpretation. The pretest data are displayed in Figure 2.4. A cursory look of the pretest data (left side of the diagram) shows little difference between what one might expect from a conventional grade book showing a list of names and test scores. However, the teacher sorts the data to render the information more useful (right side of the diagram). Follow the four steps to sort data.

1. Select the range A12:B31 using either the mouse or the keyboard.
2. Select the **Data** menu, then the **Sort** submenu.
3. Choose **Geometry** from the **Sort By** pull-down menu and the **Ascending** button.
4. Hit **OK**.

The test scores are now sorted in ascending order. In addition to identifying students from low to high scores, the sorted information easily helps the teacher to view the test score distribution.

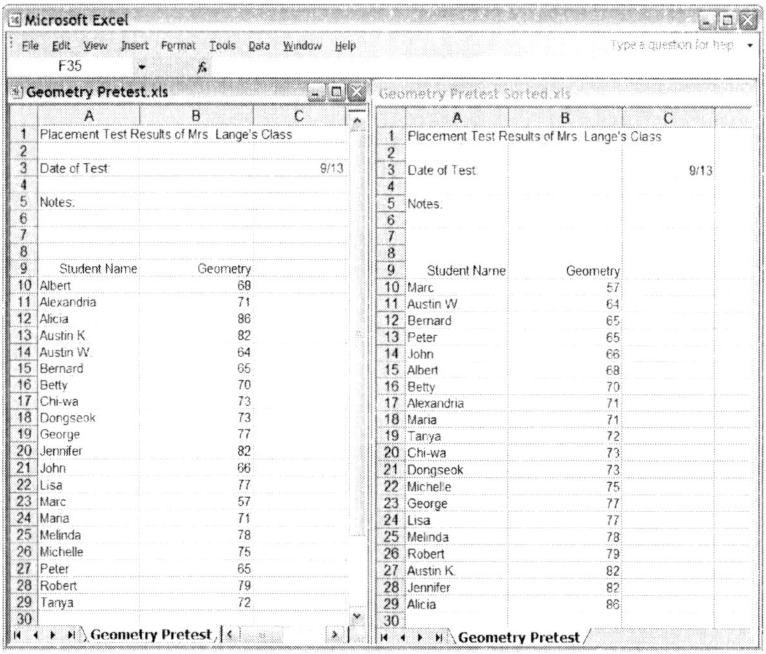

Figure 2.4. Geometry Pretest Unsorted Data (left), Sorted Data (right)

It is clear to the teacher that the students have different levels of prior knowledge based on the pretest results. For that reason, a one-size-fits-all method of instruction will not help the students to reach their individual learning needs. The teacher understands that instruction must be differentiated to be effective for a class with such academic diversity. What is differentiated instruction? Differentiated instruction means creating multiple paths so that students with different abilities, interests, or learning needs may have equal access to learn. Differentiation also allows students to take greater responsibility for their learning, and provides opportunities for peer collaboration. There are many ways to differentiate instruction; nevertheless, tiering is what the teacher uses for her mathematics class. Tiering is one common differentiated instructional strategy that teaches one key concept using varying level of complexity. There is no set number of tiers; however, three levels are often reasonable. In differentiation the key lesson concept is to be kept clear and serves as the lesson's anchor. The following diagram illustrates an application of the key concept of tiering in a mathematics lesson.

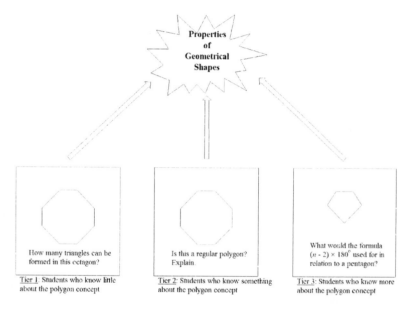

Properties of Geometrical Shapes

How many triangles can be formed in this octagon?

Is this a regular polygon? Explain.

What would the formula $(n - 2) \times 180°$ used for in relation to a pentagon?

Tier 1: Students who know little about the polygon concept

Tier 2: Students who know something about the polygon concept

Tier 3: Students who know more about the polygon concept

The tiered activity in this sample lesson focuses on the properties of geometrical shapes but the lesson follows three paths of varying degree of complexity. The basic principles targeted in the lesson may be the same, but two students may approach the principles from different directions and depth. Consequently, each student has the opportunity to learn with appropriate support and challenges. Tiering empowers the teacher to respond effectively to the diversity of multi-ability classrooms. The teacher facilitates the learning integration of students with diverse abilities. She allows students to acquire key concepts through multiple means and accommodates a variety of teaching and learning styles. Finally, she avoids assignments that are too challenging or too easy.

Student tier identification is pivotal to effective differentiated instruction and the identification for a class of twenty students is a task. For student tier identification the teacher uses a test score histogram. Excel provides the histogram feature in its Analysis ToolPak. To access the Analysis ToolPak tools, select **Data Analysis** on the **Tools** menu. If the **Data Analysis** command is not available, then you need to load the Analysis ToolPak add-in program using the following three steps.

1. On the **Tools**, select the **Add-ins** submenu.
2. Check the **Analysis ToolPak** box in the **Add-ins available** list.
3. Follow the installation instructions.

A histogram is similar to a bar graph. It shows the number of occurrences that fall in each test score interval (called a *bin*). The teacher uses a histogram to understand the relative distribution of test scores. To construct the histogram in Excel, the teacher needs to first identify the bins. A bin is like a container or holder. For convenience, the teacher uses bins with an increment of 5 points. The first bin, for example, is 46 to 50, the second bin is 51 to 55, the third bin is 56 to 60, and so on. The last bin goes from 86 to 90. The teacher enters the upper score boundaries (50, 55, 60 . . . 95, 100) of the bins on a separate column (D12:D21) in the Excel worksheet. Then the teacher follows the five steps to construct the histogram.

1. On the **Tools**, select the **Data Analysis** submenu. Then select the **Histogram** command.
2. Enter B12:B31 in the **Input Range**; enter D12:D22 in the **Bin Range**.
3. Select the **New Worksheet Ply** button, enter the name *Geometry Pretest Histogram*.
4. Check the **Chart Ouput** box.
5. Hit **OK**.

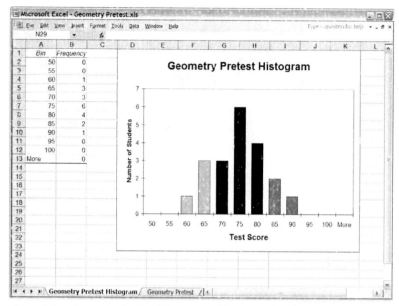

Figure 2.5.   Geometry Pretest Histogram with Instructional Groups

The results are shown in Figure 2.5: Geometry Pretest Histogram worksheet. The teacher then customizes the title, the axis labels, and so on. In addition to the frequency table in the upper left corner, a histogram chart is shown. The bins are on the horizontal axis and the numbers of occurrences are on vertical axis. The bins are labeled using their upper score boundaries. The height of the bar represents the number of occurrences. For example, the bin labeled 75 is for test score between 71 and 75 inclusively. There are six students in this bin.

The teacher identifies three groups (A, B, and C) of students with different level of test performance. There are 4 (20 percent) students in Group C. Their test scores are 65 or less. There are 13 (65 percent) students in Group B. Their test scores are greater than 65 but less than or equal to 80. There are 3 (15 percent) students in Group A. Their test scores are 81 or above.

By referencing the sorted test scores, the teacher places Marc, Austin W., and Bernard into Group C; she places Austin K., Jennifer, and Alicia into Group A; and finally she places the remaining students into Group B. Can one imagine the task of placing students into instructional groups with no data support? Keep in mind that the student groups created in the example are flexible and they are not meant to be permanent. A teacher may want to regroup the students when he is prepared to teach a new unit of study. In other words, the teacher should not use the same student groups for the geometry unit and the measurement unit for the simple reason that the readiness and interest of the student may vary for the units.

When the school principal inquires of the teacher about the progress of her mathematics class she quickly brings forward a comparison between her pre- and posttest report (Figure 2.6). The graph shows that there is growth movement in student learning from before the instruction (pretest) to the learning after the instruction (posttest). One can readily see the student learning change as represented by the bars from low to high performance over time. This claim of improvement can be further justified by comparing the means of the pretest and the posttest scores. Use the following four steps to compute means or AVERAGE in Excel.

1. Move the cursor to an empty cell anywhere in the worksheet.
2. Enter =AVERAGE(B10:B29) (see Figure 2.4 for locations of pretest test scores).
3. Hit **OK**.
4. Repeat steps 1–3 for posttest test scores.

The pretest test score mean is 72.55 and the posttest test score mean is 75.85. The pre- and posttest has a 3.30-point difference. The teacher believes in the pedagogical benefits of tiering. However, the teacher hesitates to make any firm conclusion before she reaffirms the growth findings with her other fourth-grade colleague using the same curriculum and instructional strategy. The collaboration of one teacher with another in this case serves two purposes. The first one is being a professional teacher; the second one is to roll up class data to become grade-level data for additional analysis.

The pretest–posttest comparison is a good model for measuring instructional program effectiveness when the focus of effectiveness is student achievement. Many programs such as Title I funded reading and mathematics and the federal funded ELL programs require meticulous student achievement monitoring to justify continuous program support.

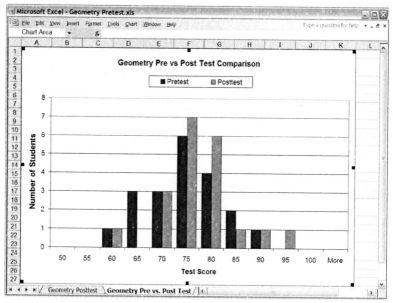

Figure 2.6.   Geometry Pretest and Posttest Comparison

STUDENT ACHIEVEMENT II: A ROLL-UP
MEASURE OF SUCCESS

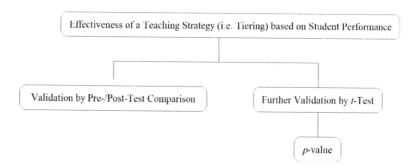

Whether you want to improve classroom achievement or schoolwide achievement, the methodology is similar. The thinking behind improving a classroom and a school is similar in that both have to maximize the success of students. Dr. Luweenski is the principal of Washington Elementary School. He knows the strengths and weaknesses of the school, the staff, and the programs through substantial data analysis. He is cognizant about the overall improvement of students with special reference to the two fourth-grade classes headed by Mrs. Lange and Mr. Peter. The principal wants to be certain that the fourth-grade students meet and exceed the state NCLB requirements as the school heads toward 100-percent proficiency. Previous state test reports of Washington School indicated that fourth-grade student performance is marginal in mathematics. A mathematics test item analysis revealed that geometry is the weak link for several years in a row. Over the summer break, fourth-grade teachers Mrs. Lange and Mr. Peter attended a regional teacher conference to learn and use the differentiated instruction strategy. A few months into the school year, the effectiveness of differentiated instruction as measured by student achievement is scrutinized.

Earlier in the mathematics test data of a class are examined in isolation. Nevertheless, the results of the two classes have to be combined to show the holistic grade-level achievement picture. When data are combined it is a roll-up. Using the Excel AVERAGE function, they calculate the following mean test scores:

	Pretest Score	Posttest Score	Improvement
Mr. Peter	71.91	73.41	1.50
Mrs. Lange	72.55	75.85	3.30
Combined	72.21	74.57	2.36

In addition, they use Excel to produce the following histograms in Figure 2.7 to compare the score distribution (the difference between the pre- and posttest scores).

Figure 2.7 shows positive score improvement. The improvement is stronger in Mrs. Lange's class than in Mr. Peter's class. However, the teachers question whether the instructional method alone makes the improvement. What could be the other contributing variables? Could this be the score criterion used in placing students into tiers? The teachers wonder if the tiering placement procedure might mix in with the teaching method to influence the student achievement. They feel that whatever conclusion they may draw, it has to be supported by additional test evidence.

To seek further test data evidence an independent samples t-test is used. The t-test is a popular statistical method that was introduced in 1908 by "Student" (the pseudonym of W.S. Gosset). Data analysts

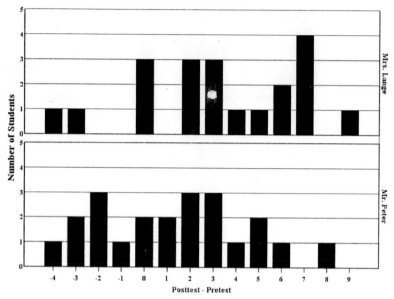

Figure 2.7.   Score Improvement Histogram

and statisticians have been using this method for the past century. This method produces one index, called the p-value (to be explained later), that helps to determine whether there is significant difference between means of the two groups, provided other variables are held constant. There are two kinds of t-test: the independent samples t-test and the paired samples t-test. The independent samples t-test is used when the two groups are considered unrelated. An example is to compare math pretest scores between students from two different classes. Students in each class form a group. The paired samples t-test is used when the two groups are considered related. An example is to compare math pretest scores and math posttest scores of students from two classes combined. The math pretest scores form a group, and the math posttest scores form the other group. The "paired" means that every student should have a math pretest score and a math posttest score.

Mr. Peter then asks the instructor how he can find out if a t-test is conclusive or not. The instructor introduces a general statistical index called the p-value (short for probability value). It is a number between zero and one inclusively. It indicates how likely that the observed difference of means is only due to chance and nothing else. When the *p*-value is small, there is weak evidence that the observed difference is only due to chance. In other words, there is strong evidence that the observed difference is due to something other than chance. When this happens, statisticians call the t-test significant. Data analysts and statisticians routinely use 0.05 (or 5 percent) as a *p*-value cutoff value. A t-test is significant when the *p*-value is less than 0.05. Otherwise, the t-test is not significant.

The instructor also explains to Mr. Peter that there are two types of *p*-value: one-tailed and two-tailed. The one-tailed *p*-value is used when the sign (plus or minus) of the observed difference matters. An example is to test whether the posttest score is higher than the pretest score. The two-tailed *p*-value is used when the sign of the difference does not matter for testing. Mr. Peter thinks the two-tailed *p*-value is sufficient for his purpose. Finally, the instructor points out to Mr. Peter that the Excel TTEST function can calculate the *p*-value of the independent samples t-test and the paired samples t-test methods. This function has four parameters. The first two parameters are the cell ranges of data to be compared. The third parameter is for the type of *p*-value: 1 for one-tailed and 2 for two-tailed. The fourth parameter is for the type of t-test: 1 for paired t-test, 2 for independent samples t-test with equal variance assumption, and 3 for independent samples t-test without equal variance assumption. The instructor suggests using the third type unless Mr. Peter is confident that students in both classes are homogeneous in terms of geometry abilities.

Mrs. Lange and Mr. Peter are excited to get this advice. They first organize the data and administer the t-test using the following steps:

1. Enter the pretest and the posttest scores for Mr. Peter's class into the ranges C2:C23 and D2:D23 respectively.
2. Enter the pretest and the posttest scores for Mrs. Lange's class into the ranges C24:C43 and D24:D43 respectively.
3. Improvements in scores are calculated by subtracting column C from column D and put results into column E (see Figure 2.8).

To execute the independent sample t-test for comparing the pretest scores between the two classes, the following Excel function statements are used. The resulting *p*-values are listed alongside.

Using the *p*-value cutoff of 0.05, Mrs. Lange and Mr. Peter conclude that no independent samples t-tests are significant. In other words,

Mr. Peter				Mrs. Lange			
Student Name	Geometry Pretest	Geometry Posttest	Posttest - Pretest	Student Name	Geometry Pretest	Geometry Posttest	Posttest - Pretest
Alan	69	69	0	Albert	68	68	0
Albert	72	77	5	Alexandria	71	74	3
Amber	86	84	-2	Alicia	86	95	9
Beatrice	70	73	3	Austin K.	82	82	0
Charles	69	67	-2	Austin W.	64	70	6
Chi-Ko	79	82	3	Bernard	65	72	7
Derek	62	61	-1	Betty	70	77	7
Elaine	72	70	-2	Chi-wa	73	80	7
Elizabeth	83	83	0	Dongseok	73	80	7
Ellen	58	55	-3	George	77	74	-3
Flora	69	71	2	Jennifer	82	87	5
George	64	68	4	John	66	69	3
Herbert	69	72	3	Lisa	77	77	0
Ibrahim	61	66	5	Marc	57	60	3
Iris	84	92	8	Maria	71	75	4
Joseph	86	83	-3	Melinda	78	80	2
Karen	60	61	1	Michelle	75	77	2
Mario	72	73	1	Peter	65	71	6
Mei-Ling	76	82	6	Robert	79	75	-4
Molly	72	74	2	Tanya	72	74	2
Monica	76	72	-4				
Winnie	73	75	2				

Figure 2.8.   Geometry Pretest and Posttest Scores of Fourth-Grade Students

Comparison of ...	Excel Function Statement	*p*-value
Pretest scores between the two classes	=TTEST(C2:C23,C24:C43,2,3)	0.7883
Posttest scores between the two classes	=TTEST(D2:D23,D24:D43,2,3)	0.3353
Score improvements between the two classes	=TTEST(E2:E23,D24:D43,2,3)	0.0930

there are no substantial differences in pretest scores, posttest scores, and score improvements between the two classes. The benefits of the tiering method apply equally to students in both classes. The difference may be due to other contributing variables.

Next, the teachers compare the pretest scores to the posttest scores for the two classes. Since both Mrs. Lange and Mr. Peter expect positive improvement in scores, they calculate the one-tailed *p*-value of the paired samples t-test using the Excel function statement: =TTEST(C2:C43,D2:D43,1,1). In order to measure their individual teaching effectiveness, they repeat the comparison for each class. The following table lists the comparisons made the Excel function statements, and the resulting *p*-values.

Comparison of ...	Excel Function Statement	*p*-value
Posttest scores to pretest scores for two classes combined	=TTEST(C2:C43,D2:D43,1,1)	0.00003
Posttest scores to pretest scores for Mrs. Lange's class	=TTEST(C24:C43,D24:D43,1,1)	0.00025
Posttest scores to pretest scores for Mr. Peter's class	=TTEST(C2:C23,D2:D23,1,1)	0.02013

Using the *p*-value cutoff of 0.05, Mrs. Lange and Mr. Peter conclude that all paired samples t-tests are significant. In other words, the posttest scores are significantly higher than the pretest scores. They attribute this finding to the impact of the tiering instructional method. The finding also suggests that this instructional method has a stronger improvement impact in Mrs. Lange's class than in Mr. Peter's class. Mr. Peter is not surprised about this finding because he has less teaching experience than Mrs. Lange.

During a staff meeting, Mrs. Lange and Mr. Peter share their findings with Dr. Luweenski, the school principal. Dr. Luweenski is thrilled to know that the tiering instructional method works well to improve students' geometry achievement. Out of curiosity, Dr. Luweenski asks the teachers whether students in the free or reduced lunch program show a similar achievement improvement like their peers. The principal brings up this question because disaggregation of achievement into student subgroups such as students with free and reduced lunch is a criterion of the NCLB law (see Figure 2.9).

The teachers go back to the Excel spreadsheet and add a new column G to identify the free and reduced lunch students. A value *Yes* shows a student in the program, and *No* otherwise. There are six free and reduced lunch students out of forty.

The teachers choose the independent samples t-test method for comparing the two groups of students. Since they do not expect the difference, if any, in any direction, they calculate the two-tailed *p*-value. They follow the three steps below:

1. Select the **Data** menu, then the **Sort** command to sort the entire worksheet by the column G in descending order. Students in the program are on rows 2 to 7. Other students are on rows 8 to 43.

Teacher	Student Name	Geometry Pretest	Geometry Posttest	Posttest - Pretest	Free or Reduced Lunch?
Mr. Peter	Ellen	58	55	-3	Yes
Mr. Peter	Karen	60	61	1	Yes
Mrs. Lange	Albert	68	68	0	Yes
Mrs. Lange	John	66	69	3	Yes
Mrs. Lange	Marc	57	60	3	Yes
Mrs. Lange	Peter	65	71	6	Yes
Mr. Peter	Alan	69	69	0	No
Mr. Peter	Albert	72	77	5	No
Mr. Peter	Amber	86	84	-2	No
Mr. Peter	Beatrice	70	73	3	No
Mr. Peter	Charles	69	67	-2	No
Mr. Peter	Chi-Ko	79	82	3	No
Mr. Peter	Derek	62	61	-1	No
Mr. Peter	Elaine	72	70	-2	No
Mr. Peter	Elizabeth	83	83	0	No
Mr. Peter	Flora	69	71	2	No
Mr. Peter	George	64	68	4	No
Mr. Peter	Herbert	69	72	3	No

Figure 2.9. Geometry Pretest and Posttest Scores Sorted by Free or Reduced Lunch Participation Indicator

2. Use the function = AVERAGE(E2:E7) to calculate the average improvement for students in the program, and the function = AVERAGE(E8:E43) for other students.
3. Use the function = TTEST(E2:E7,E8:E43,2,3) to calculate the two-tailed *p*-value for the independent samples t-test.

Means of the score improvement for both groups are displayed:

Free or Reduced Lunch Program	Improvement
Yes	1.67
No	2.47

Although the free or reduced lunch students show smaller improvement than the regular paid lunch students, the two-tailed *p*-value of 0.5787 suggests that there is little support to show that a student status in the lunch program influences the test score difference. Research has shown that a student's social economic status as measured by the participation of the free and reduced lunch program is normally a good predictor of student academic success. What happened to the achievement of Mrs. Lange's and Mr. Peter's free and reduced lunch students? These students show improvement alongside peers pointing to the instructional effectiveness of the teachers. The teachers are the motivators and the enablers and they are key to student success.

CHAPTER REFLECTION

1. What are the key components of an effective attendance record?
2. What are the variables affecting student attendance and over which of those variables do we have no or little control? Why?
3. Why is it crucial to keep accurate student attendance records?
4. Your record shows a problem in student attendance. How would you develop an improvement plan to solve the problem? Please explain.
5. How do you identify the academic readiness of your students? Please describe the identification strategy.
6. How do you address the academic diversity of your students effectively? Please use a lesson plan to illustrate.
7. What is student data disaggregation and how does it apply to meeting the requirements of the NCLB law?
8. Describe a situation in which you analyze student data trends over time to determine the strengths and weaknesses of an academic program for the purpose of improvement.
9. How do you differentiate the use of a t-test and the determination of p-value to determine the effectiveness of a teaching strategy? Please use an example to illustrate.
10. What might be the relationship between student attendance and learning and how do you prove or disprove your hypothesis?

3

School Professional Practice and Program Data, Improvement, and Accountability: Professional Practice: Walk-through Supervision and Collaborative Coaching

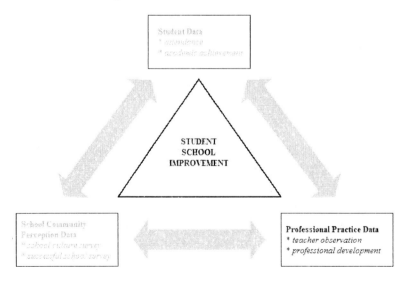

School improvement simply means the increase of student success. The task of improvement usually rests on the shoulders of the school principal. Certain expectations are imposed on the school principal regardless of the quality and support of the school staff, including all aspects of school leadership, such as instructional improvement and staff and program assessment. With the demanding task of improvement, many schools are taking on the challenge using a team approach. A school improvement team is created to garner input from the teaching staff, the supporting staff, parents, citizens, and students for improvement efforts.

Teacher assessment is an important task in a school improvement process because teachers hold the key to making student learning happen. The purpose of teacher assessment has to be clear to both the evaluator and the evaluatee to lend the process valid and productive. The kind of assessment that we are going to discuss is formative in nature. Formative assessment is directed toward helping the teacher to improve, and it should not be threatening or affect critical decisions such as tenure and job retention. A typical formative assessment report is anecdotal and describes the behavior of the person observed. Put yourself in the shoes of a school principal and walk in his or her shoes for a day. Can you imagine the time a principal spends in the office, the classrooms, the lunchroom, the hallway, the playground, the bus stop, and all the other places in between from dawn to dusk? How much time would a school principal spend in observing teaching and learning when his or her role is to be the school instructional leader? The overcommitted principal will probably tell you that he or she would be lucky to spend 50 percent of the work time in the classrooms. The time a principal uses to visit a class is very limited and precious. Often unscheduled meetings and troubleshooting around the school interrupt the classroom visit. For that reason, the principal should maximize each classroom visit to observe, to record, and to suggest ways to improve teachers.

Collaborative coaching is another way that two teachers will work together for improvement. Collaborative coaching provides a low-risk opportunity for a veteran teacher (sometimes called a mentor) to work in a nonjudgmental, interactive fashion. The collaboration occurs when the teachers discuss what will be observed and what data collected during the visit. The purpose of collaborative coaching is to foster self-reflection and self-analysis in a safe environment where ideas for growth are shared. Any two teachers who agree to be partners in a collaborative coaching experience are all we need for the process. It includes a preconference, an observation, and a postconference where both teachers take an active role in sharing information.

There are many things that a school principal or a mentor teacher can record in an informal classroom visit. Nevertheless, there are two variables important to improve students. They drive student learning, and the teacher can control them. Classroom management is the first variable, traditionally referred to as student discipline. Actually, classroom management goes beyond student discipline to include the rules and consequences, the classroom atmosphere, the relationship between the students and the adult, and of course the proper learning behavior of the students. The second one is instruction, and it includes a wide variety of teacher behaviors, including the interaction between the teacher and the students, the structure of the lesson, the prioritization of the skills and concepts taught, the high expectation of teachers toward the students, the appropriate use of instructional materials, and so on. The following two figures, on pages 49 to 51, illustrate the performance indicators at different levels regarding classroom management and effective instruction. As we go from the left to the right hand side of the chart, we see a progression of teachers' skills. This skill progression is described as emerging, applying, integrating, and innovating. The four levels of expertise are correlated to the training as well as the experience of the teacher as shown in Figure 3.1.

To facilitate a brief fifteen-minute or less classroom visit and obtain as much information as possible, a walk-through checklist (page 52) is developed. The checklist is a data-gathering tool and technique that is essential for working with teachers to improve teaching. It provides reflective feedback to maximize student learning. The checklist is an Excel spreadsheet with a standardized format. It shows the header row of the checklist and it has the following thirteen items.

Items 1 through 5 are basic identification information. Items 6 through 8 are related to student management with item 9 as the summary of the three management items. Items 10 through 12 are related to instruction with item 13 as the summary of the four instruction items. When the administrator walks through the classroom, the focus of the visit is classroom management and instruction. For each separate item under classroom management and instruction, the checklist assigns a number to each of the four levels of proficiency: 1 = emerging, 2 = applying, 3 = integrating, and 4 = innovating.

Figure 3.3 shows that Mr. Peter, a new teacher, has been visited by the principals seven times in September and five times in October. On the other hand, Mrs. Lange, a tenured teacher has been visited six times between September and October.

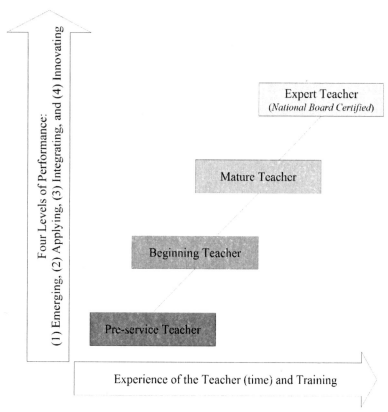

Figure 3.1. Skill Progression of a Career Teacher

The checklist (figure 3.3) indicates that on September 2, Mr. Peter's *average score for management* is 2 based on the mean of the three management subscores (1, 3, and 2) listed. The average score of 2 indicates that Mr. Peter does not meet the proficiency, and he is in need of improvement. About a month later, the average score for management shows an improved score of 3.33. Mr. Peter has improved his classroom management skills, and it is backed by the average score increase. It is apparent from the chart that Mr. Peter's biggest improvement (i.e., from a 1 to 4) is in establishing law and order in the classroom. The supervisor (principal) can reference the change of data over time and make appropriate suggestions for improvement. Making suggestions for improvement based on isolated data is always risky. To establish a trend one needs to take a careful longitudinal

Figure 3.2.

Performance Indicators for Classroom Management

Performance Description	(1) Emerging	(2) Applying	(3) Integrating	(4) Innovating
Class is safe and orderly	*Communicates expectations and consequences for student behavior.*	*Uses strategies that prevent or lessen disruptive expectations for behavior.*	*Reinforces expectations and consequences, and supports students to monitor their own behavior and each other's in a respectful way.*	*Facilitates a positive environment in which students are guided to take a strong role in communicating, maintaining, and monitoring behavior.*
	Responds appropriately to disruptive behavior and promotes some positive.	*Monitors behavior while teaching and during student work time.*		
Student and staff are respectful of each other	*Establishes rapport with students.*	*Promotes caring and respectful interactions.*	*Maintains caring and respectful relationships with students.*	*Fosters a safe and inclusive learning community.*
	Acknowledges some incidents of unfairness and disrespect.	*Responds to incidents of unfairness and disrespect.*	*Supports students in developing skills to respond to unfairness and disrespect.*	*Students participate in maintaining a climate of respect and may initiate creative solutions to conflicts.*
		Encourages students to respect differences.		
Students on tasks	*Provides time for students to complete learning activities.*	*Provides adequate time for presentation and for completion of learning activities.*	*Paces instruction to include ongoing review and closure of lessons to connect them to future lessons.*	*Presents, adjusts, and facilitates instruction and daily activities so all students have time for learning are continually engaged, and have opportunities for reflection and assessment.*
	Develops some routines classroom.	*Paces instruction to maintain engagement.*	*Classroom transitions are efficient and integrated into learning activities.*	
	Uses strategies to pace and adjust instruction to insure continual engagement.	*Uses transitions to support engagement of all students.*		

Performance Indicators for Instruction

Performance Description	(1) Emerging	(2) Applying	(3) Integrating	(4) Innovating
Concepts are clear and prioritized	Has a basic knowledge of subject matter and student development. Promotes an understanding of key concepts.	Communicates key concepts, skills in an accurate and clear manner. Builds on instruction with students' cognitive abilities in mind.	Uses expanded knowledge of subject matter to support student understanding of concepts. Activities are suitable for students' cognitive development.	Flexibly uses comprehensive knowledge of subject matter and student development to ensure that all students understand key concepts.
Teaching is interactive	Maintains regular communication with all students. Uses questioning techniques for yes and no responses.	Engages students in classroom interaction. Students respond to simple questions.	Uses verbal and non-verbal techniques to manage behavior, make expectations clear, and motivates learning.	Uses questioning techniques that stimulate students to think critically and formulate their own thinking. Uses effective responsive listening skills to guide classroom interaction.
Instruction is developmentally appropriate	Provides time for students to complete learning activities. Uses strategies to pace and adjust instruction to insure continual engagement.	Provides adequate time for presentation and for completion of learning activities. Paces instruction to maintain engagement. Use transitions to support engagement of all students.	Paces instruction to include ongoing review and closure of lessons to connect them to future lessons. Classroom transitions are efficient and integrated into learning activities.	Presents, adjusts, and facilitates instruction and daily activities so all students have time for learning are continually engaged, and have opportunities for reflection and assessment.

Performance Indicators for Instruction (continued)

Performance Description	(1) Emerging	(2) Applying	(3) Integrating	(4) Innovating
Use of supportive instructional materials	Uses available instructional materials, resources, and technologies for specific lessons to support student learning.	Selects and uses appropriate instructional materials, resources, and technologies to present concepts and skills. Materials reflect diversity students. Resources are made available to all students.	Selects, adapts, and creates a range of relevant materials, resources, and technologies to enrich learning, to reflect cultural diversity of students, and to provide equal access.	Analyzes, adapts, and creates a wide range of relevant instructional materials, resources, and technologies to extend students' understanding and provide equal access. Materials reflect diversity beyond the classroom.

Identification Information	(1) The date of visit
	(2) The last name of the teacher
	(3) The first name of the teacher
	(4) The grade level
	(5) The subject matter taught
Classroom Management	(6) Class is safe and orderly
	(7) Students and staff treat each other with respect
	(8) Students are on task
	(9) Average Score for Management
Instruction	(10) Concepts are clear and prioritized
	(11) Instruction is developmentally appropriate
	(12) Effective use of support materials
	(13) Average Score for Instruction

STAFF ASSESSMENT WALK-THROUGH CHECKLIST
(original data)

Visit date	Teacher	Grade	Subject	Class is safe & orderly	Students and staff treat each other with respect	Students are on task	Average Score for Management	Concepts are clear and prioritized	Teaching is interactive	Instruction is develomentally appropriate	Effective use of support materials	Average Score for Instructio
09/02	John Peter	4	Math	1	3	2	2.00	2	2	1	2	1.75
09/06	Maria Lange	4	Math	3	4	4	3.67	3	4	4	4	3.75
09/07	John Peter	4	Math	2	2	2	2.00	2	2	1	2	1.75
09/08	Maria Lange	4	Math	3	2	3	2.67	4	3	2	4	3.25
09/10	John Peter	4	Math	2	2	3	2.33	1	2	2	2	1.75
09/15	John Peter	4	Math	1	2	1	1.33	2	1	3	2	2.00
09/16	John Peter	4	Math	3	2	3	2.67	2	2	3	2	2.25
09/22	Maria Lange	4	Math	3	4	4	3.67	4	3	3	4	3.50
09/24	John Peter	4	Math	3	2	2	2.33	3	1	2	3	2.25
09/30	John Peter	4	Math	3	4	1	2.67	3	2	3	4	3.00
10/04	John Peter	4	Math	2	2	4	2.67	3	2	2	3	2.50
10/05	Maria Lange	4	Math	3	4	4	3.67	3	2	4	4	3.25
10/07	John Peter	4	Math	3	2	4	3.00	3	3	3	2	2.75
10/14	Maria Lange	4	Math	4	4	4	4.00	4	4	4	3	3.75
10/15	John Peter	4	Math	3	4	3	3.33	3	3	3	4	3.25
10/21	John Peter	4	Math	4	4	3	3.67	4	4	3	3	3.50
10/22	Maria Lange	4	Math	4	4	3	3.67	3	4	3	3	3.50
10/25	John Peter	4	Math	4	3	3	3.33	4	4	4	3	3.75

(sorted by Teacher name, Average Score for Management, and Average Score for Instruction)

Visit date	Teacher	Grade	Subject	Class is safe & orderly	Students and staff treat each other with respect	Students are on task	Average Score for Management	Concepts are clear and prioritized	Teaching is interactive	Instruction is develomentally appropriate	Effective use of support materials	Average Score fo Instructi
09/15	John Peter	4	Math	1	2	1	1.33	2	1	3	2	2.00
09/02	John Peter	4	Math	1	3	2	2.00	2	2	1	2	1.75
09/07	John Peter	4	Math	2	2	2	2.00	2	2	1	2	1.75
09/10	John Peter	4	Math	2	2	3	2.33	1	2	2	2	1.75
09/24	John Peter	4	Math	3	2	2	2.33	3	1	2	3	2.25
09/16	John Peter	4	Math	3	2	3	2.67	2	2	3	2	2.25
10/04	John Peter	4	Math	2	2	4	2.67	3	2	2	3	2.50
09/30	John Peter	4	Math	3	4	1	2.67	3	2	3	4	3.00
10/07	John Peter	4	Math	3	2	4	3.00	3	3	3	2	2.75
10/15	John Peter	4	Math	3	4	3	3.33	3	3	3	4	3.25
10/25	John Peter	4	Math	4	3	3	3.33	4	4	4	3	3.75
10/21	John Peter	4	Math	4	4	3	3.67	4	4	3	3	3.50
09/08	Maria Lange	4	Math	3	2	3	2.67	4	3	2	4	3.25
10/05	Maria Lange	4	Math	3	4	4	3.67	3	2	4	4	3.25
09/22	Maria Lange	4	Math	3	4	4	3.67	4	3	3	4	3.50
10/22	Maria Lange	4	Math	4	4	3	3.67	3	4	3	3	3.50
09/06	Maria Lange	4	Math	3	4	4	3.67	3	4	4	4	3.75
10/14	Maria Lange	4	Math	4	4	4	4.00	4	4	4	3	3.75

Figure 3.2. Staff Assessment Checklist Unsorted and Sorted Data Comparison

Visit Date	Teacher	Grade	Subject	Class if safe and orderly	Students and staff treat each other with respect	Students are on task	Average Score for Management
09/02	John Peter	4	Math	1	3	2	2.00
10/25	John Peter	4	Math	4	3	3	3.33

Figure 3.3. An Assessment of Mr. Peter's Classroom Management Skills

look at the data set. The visitation data from September 2 to October 25 are a data set. What data trend do you see? Is Mr. Peter fine with classroom management? What is the relationship between teaching effectiveness and classroom management?

There are practical tips for using the assessment checklist appropriately and they are:

1. Communicate with the union people and make them understand and agree on the purpose of the assessment checklist.
2. Communicate with the teacher regularly about the walkthrough and make sure that mutual understanding and trust are firmly established. Make timely feedbacks to teachers regarding strengths and weaknesses.
3. The principal may initially inform, as professional courtesy, the teacher about the visit. Nevertheless, the process should become more informal as the visitation gradually becomes a walkthrough routine. In the case of collaborative coaching, have the teachers agree on two or three mutually convenient visitation dates.
4. Try not to bring the checklist on a clipboard while visiting the class. This may give the teacher the intimidating impression of judging and not helping.
5. Do not rely on the information from just a few visits to make improvement recommendations. Visit more than a few times to establish a trend before making appropriate suggestions.
6. You do not have to observe an entire lesson to appraise effectiveness. Schedule your visits to observe the beginning of the lesson, the middle of the lesson, then the end session of the lesson to formulate the trends of behavior.
7. Ask reflective questions and stay positive. The principal or mentor might say, "I know you like to reflect on your teaching. When I was in the class, I noticed you were working with cooperative

learning groups." The critical attributes to such a statement are, first, it is not negative, and second, it focuses on the teaching.

8. Embed the Excel function of AVERAGE in the *average score for management* cell so the computation of the average score is automatic every time numbers are entered in the cells. Repeat the AVERAGE function in the *average score for instruction* cell. Then the computation of the average scores would be just as easy.

PROGRAM EVALUATION I: ENGLISH LANGUAGE LEARNER PROGRAM

[Program assessment is a common education practice to determine the success of the curriculum, the instruction, and the impact on student learning.) How does a textbook selection committee recommend a social studies pilot text for adoption? How does the curriculum director know that the summer remedial reading class is effective in helping students to retain and make advances in reading comprehension strategies? How does the gifted and talented program coordinator justify the continuous subscription of a computer-assisted instruction program? The answer to these questions resides in what we understand from the program assessment data. In Chapter 2, the method of pre- and posttest comparison is presented and discussed. While the pre- and posttest comparison is a common valid assessment method, nonetheless, a different tool called the PivotTable in Excel is introduced in this chapter. A pivot table is an interactive Excel worksheet table that quickly summarizes large amounts of data using calculation methods you choose. It is called a pivot table because you can rotate its row and column headings around the core data area to give you different views of the source data. Let us examine how an instructional program such as English Language Learner (ELL) is being evaluated.

State- and federal-funded programs are accountable to regular monitoring with reference to student achievement. The monitoring is a report with student data, and it usually occurs at the end of the school year. The ELL program in the past has been given different names such as the Bilingual Education program or the English as a Second Language (ESL) program. The ELL program serviced students with low English-language proficiency, who are sometimes called the limited English proficient (LEP) students.

A new student upon admission to a school system is given the Home Language Survey Test (Figure 3.4). It is a new student admission legal requirement. When a student's home language is not

STUDENT

Home Language Survey

Administer to ALL new students

Woodcock Munoz Test for English Proficiency

Administer to all eligible students.
Students are placed in 1 - 5 proficiency level with parent consent.

Student Placement

Students in <u>Level 1</u> (beginning/preproduction)
<u>Level 2</u> (beginning/production)
<u>Level 3</u> (intermediate)
are placed in direct ESL instruction schools upon the
consent of the parent/guardian

Students in <u>Level 4</u> (advanced intermediate)
<u>Level 5</u> (advanced)
will receive indirect ESL instruction upon the consent
of the parent/guardian

Figure 3.4. English Language Learner Students' Identification and Placement
Note: ESL = English as a Second Language.

English, or if the student's communication outside the school or at home is not English, the student will be asked to take an English proficiency test. The Woodcock-Munoz Language Survey and the Language Assessment Scale are examples of English-proficiency tests. A student with a low proficiency score (i.e., proficiency level 1 to 3) will be placed to receive direct instruction or from a certified ESL instructor. A student with a higher proficiency level of 4 and 5 will receive monitored instruction under the jurisdiction of a regular education teacher and an ESL teacher. A description of the proficiency level is given below.

Level 1: Beginning/preproduction. The student does not understand or speak English with the exception of a few isolated words or expressions.

Level 2: Beginning/production. The student understands and speaks conversational and academic English with hesitancy and difficulty. The student understands parts of lessons and simple directions. The student is at a preemergent or emergent level of reading and writing in English, significantly below grade level.

Level 3: Intermediate. The student understands and speaks conversational and academic English with decreasing hesitancy and difficulty. The student is postemergent, developing reading comprehension and writing skills in English. The student's English literacy skills allow the student to demonstrate academic knowledge in content areas with assistance.

Level 4: Advanced intermediate. The student understands and speaks conversational English without apparent difficulty but understands and speaks academic English with some hesitancy. The student continues to acquire reading and writing skills in content areas needed to achieve grade-level expectations with assistance.

Level 5: Advanced. The student understands and speaks conversational and academic English well. The student is near proficient in reading, writing, and content area skills needed to meet grade level expectations. The student requires occasional support.

Level 6: Formerly LEP/Now fully English proficient. The student was formerly LEP and is now fully English proficient. The student understands, speaks, reads, and writes English, and possesses thinking and reasoning skills to succeed in academic classes at or above the student's age or grade level.

Level 7: Fully English proficient. The student was never classified as LEP and does not fit the definition of an LEP student outlined in the No Child Left Behind Act of 2001 Title IX sec. 9101(25)(A)-(D)

Let us look at how an ESL class is evaluated using English-language proficiency as a measure. The following Excel chart shows an ESL class of twenty students with the pretest (test 1) and posttest (test 2) results. The number in the columns represents the level of English-language proficiency; 1 is low English proficiency and 5 is high English proficiency.

	A	B	C	D	E
1	ELL English Proficiency Test Data				
2					
3			English Proficiency		
4	Student	Ethnicity	Test 1	Test 2	
5	Jose K	Mexico	1	2	
6	Soon	Korea	1	1	
7	Russ	Poland	1	3	
8	Jose G	Mexico	2	3	
9	Maria	Spain	2	3	
10	David	Germany	2	2	
11	Pham	Vietnam	2	3	
12	Pat	Costa Rica	2	3	
13	Harlan	Germany	2	3	
14	Kairy	Egypt	3	3	
15	Joe	Poland	3	4	
16	Chee	China	3	4	
17	Nancy	Russia	4	5	
18	Tracey	Sweden	4	4	
19	Ming	China	4	5	
20	Eileen	Indonesia	5	6	
21	Heather	Russia	5	6	
22					

Select the **Data** menu in Excel, then the **PivotTable and PivotChart Report** command. An interface wizard consisting of three steps shows up. Below is the first step panel. Since the data is already in the Excel spreadsheet, the default options are used.

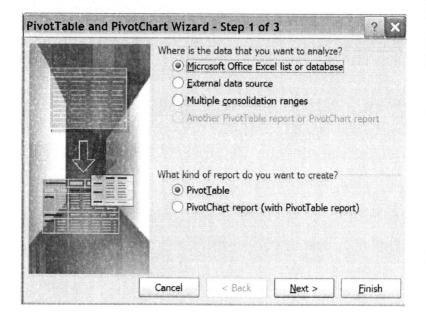

Next, cell range of the data (A4:D21) is specified in the second step panel.

Finally, the pivot table layout and its contents are specified in the third step panel. We choose to put the pivot table along with the data. The position of the pivot table is determined by its upper left corner. We assign the F4 cell to be its upper left corner.

The **Options** button opens the **PivotTable Options** dialog. Various format and data options are available in this dialog. Except changing the name in the **Name** field to ELL Program Effectiveness, the default settings are used.

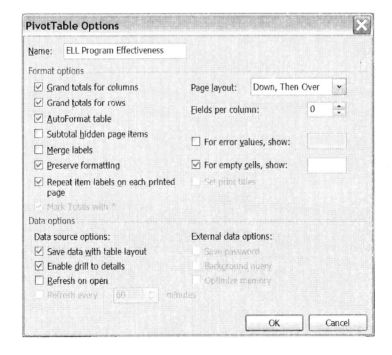

The **Layout** button opens the **PivotTable and PivotChart Wizard—Layout** dialog. This dialog is used to specify the organization of the pivot table. A pivot table has a row, a column, and cell contents.

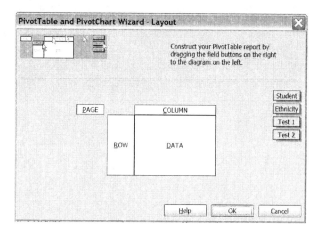

To put Test 1 in the row, use the mouse to drag the field button labeled "Test 1" in the rightmost side of the dialog to the ROW position inside the diagram. Similarly, drag the field button labeled "Test 2" to the COLUMN position to put Test 2 in the column. Finally, drag the field button labeled "Student" to the DATA position. The default cell content is count of student.

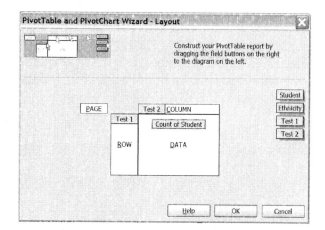

We are interested in the percents of students that moved up from the entry English-proficiency level. Therefore, we need to select a different type of cell content. To do this, we double click on the button labeled "Count of Student" to open the **PivotTable Field** dialog.

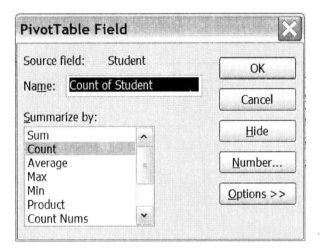

Select the **Options** button to expand the dialog. Select **% of row** from the **Show data as** selection list. In addition, put *% Row* in the **Name** field. Hit **OK** when the necessary selections and changes have been made.

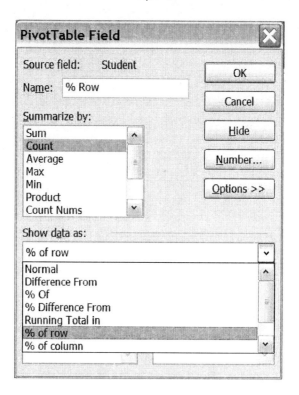

Finally, hit **Finish** in the third step panel to generate the pivot table shown below.

F	G	H	I	J	K	L	M
4 %Row	Test 2						
5 Test 1	1	2	3	4	5	6	Grand Total
6 1	33.33%	**33.33%**	**33.33%**	0.00%	0.00%	**0.00%**	100.00%
7 2	0.00%	16.67%	**83.33%**	0.00%	0.00%	**0.00%**	100.00%
8 3	0.00%	0.00%	33.33%	**66.67%**	0.00%	**0.00%**	100.00%
9 4	0.00%	0.00%	0.00%	33.33%	**66.67%**	**0.00%**	100.00%
10 5	0.00%	0.00%	0.00%	0.00%	0.00%	**100.00%**	100.00%
11 Grand Tota	5.88%	11.76%	41.18%	17.65%	11.76%	11.76%	100.00%

The results show that for English proficiency level 1 students, one-third of them remained at the same level, one-third moved up one level, and one-third moved up two levels. For English proficiency level 2 students, one-sixth of them remained at the same level, and five-sixths moved up one level.

For English proficiency level 3 students, one-third of them remained at the same level, and two-thirds moved up one level. For English proficiency level 4 students, one-third of them remained at the same level, and two-thirds moved up one level. Finally, for English proficiency level 5 students, all of them moved up one level.

To measure the success of the ELL program, we calculate the average percentages of students who have moved up at least 1 level. The Excel function statement: = AVERAGE(SUM(H6:L6),SUM(I7:L7),SUM (J8:L8),SUM(K9:L9),SUM(L10)) returns the result of 76.67 percent. This indicates that about three out of four ELL students move up at least one level.

What is the ELL adequate yearly progress (AYP) accountability? A key feature of the No Child Left Behind (NCLB) law is enforcement of AYP for all students to include ELL students. Schools must meet state-determined AYP criteria for academic progress for all students as well as subgroups of students by ethnicity, English proficiency, income level, and special education. This places a new accountability on the levels of achievement for ELL. NCLB outlines the accountability process that individual states must develop systems that measure the academic progress of all students. This process includes: setting challenging academic standards, developing annual state-level assessments that address the states' learning standards, setting an initial starting point, specifying successive targets for AYP, and providing support to schools that repeatedly do not meet AYP. Furthermore, there is constant variance in the ELL subgroup populations since students continuously transition out of ELL programs as they achieve English-language proficiency. This creates a subgroup that is continually made up of low-performing students. The U.S. Department of Education (2004) offers states an option that allows ELL students who have attained English proficiency (Level 6 and beyond) and exited an ELL program to continue to be accountable for up to two years in the ELL subgroup. This option provides states with greater flexibility for showing academic growth of ELL subgroups because students with higher levels of language proficiency and potentially higher scores would remain in the ELL subgroup count.

Teacher efficacy, within a culturally responsive classroom, is the lynch pin inherent across the effective ELL strategies of challenging instruction, teacher-student collaboration, and valuing students as learners. Teacher efficacy expands the concept of teacher expectations. Specific characteristics of an effective teacher include a teacher's personal belief that he or she can influence student learning. Teachers with high levels of efficacy also have a sense of personal commitment and see their work as purposeful and important. They take personal responsibility for their work, holding themselves accountable for student performance, and they examine their instructional practices when student performance is less than expected. Teachers who possess high levels of efficacy, who use research-based instructional models, and who provide explicit strategy instruction, can make a difference with ELL students and close the achievement gaps.

The world around us is in motion, changing at dizzying speed. To meet the needs, schools are preparing students for a profoundly different future. By midcentury, no one ethnic group will make up a significant majority of the U.S. population. By 2050, the long-standing non-Hispanic white majority will represent 53 percent of the population, down from 71 percent in 2000. Shortly after 2050, the United States will become a nation of minorities (*Ten Trends*). Providing equal opportunity and closing the achievement gap among students of various ethnic groups are among the most demanding issues facing schools at the turn of the century. This challenge to educate will be magnified by the move toward rigorous standards and high-stakes testing. Generally, schools will offer an even greater focus on running more effective ELL program.

PROGRAM EVALUATION II: PROFESSIONAL DEVELOPMENT

Why do we need to evaluate the effectiveness of a program? When the wager is high for student achievement, the priority to improve the teachers is also high. Like other professionals, teachers must keep up with the best instructional practices so they may help to improve the learning of students. Regardless of the size or the complexity of the school organization, the revitalization of staff members' professional skills is elemental to improvement (Guskey and Huberman, 1995). What is professional development? It is a purposeful, continuous, and systemic process to improve the attitude, knowledge, and skills of the educators. Professional development activities are planned with a clear purpose, what Steven Covey (1990) refers to as "begin with the end in mind." One simple example of planning with a clear goal for a school can be the training of the teaching staff to use a newly adopted English language arts program. When teachers are given a new instructional tool, we just cannot assume the teachers to know by default the philosophy, the organization, and the coordination of the strategies and the supporting resources. This void of knowledge and skills will not be effectively filled if it is not for the purposeful implementation of professional development activities. As a novice teacher adopting a new program, one single in-service session at the beginning of a school year is just the introduction. A teacher may come across challenges of applying a specific teaching technique such as literature circle as he works through the chapters of the textbook. In this case, a onetime English language arts training in September will render the teacher still helpless to sustain the school year. For that reason, an effective professional development needs to be continuous and sustainable. In many schools, several days are set aside in the school calendar for continuous professional development. On a professional development day, the students might get to finish school a few hours earlier so the school staff can get time together to learn and to share. Effective professional development is systemic. It takes into account all levels of the school organization and includes certified and support services staff.

How do we prepare to evaluate program effectiveness? When professional development is implemented systemically, the needs of the individual and the needs of the school are addressed to move the organization forward for student success. The effectiveness of professional development is often manifested by how the participants perceive the professional development programs as being useful. For that reason, participants are often asked to complete an evaluation form to poll their opinions. These forms vary in length and in complexity. Typically, ordinal rating scale items and open-ended response items are used. Participants who wish to clarify and extend their responses are encouraged to use the comments section.

In the design of a professional development evaluation form, a balance must be reached between the quality of information and the complexity of the form. Since participants are already overwhelmed with new staff development information, they may not have the attention span to complete a complex and lengthy form. On the contrary, an oversimplified form may give participants an impression that their responses are not taken seriously. Participants should be informed at the beginning of the day that there will be a survey at the end of the professional development activity. We recommend a short session, fifteen minutes for example, for the participants to complete and to return the evaluation. A bad practice is to tell the participants to pick up and complete the evaluation forms as they exit and to give them the option of returning the forms the next school day.

The first step to a successful survey is to prepare the mind-set of the participants. They must realize that providing feedback is an obligation of a professional development day; they have the trust from the district officials that honest responses are encouraged and all responses are confidential (unless the participant chooses to be identified). They will gain access to the survey summary report in a short time.

On the other hand, district officials should view the survey as an important component of the professional development day. They should spend efforts in carefully designing the questionnaires. Asking the wrong questions but not getting the wrong answers is the common mistake made in conducting a survey. A survey is destined to failure when the questionnaire is hastily put together.

Figure 3.5 is an example of a professional development evaluation form for the Silverbrook School District. It has one opening session and two breakout sessions. The format of an "item" is actually a statement of criteria. For example, "The overall effectiveness was high" is a criteria statement. The participant is asked to evaluate his or her experience against that criterion with a sliding scale of agreement to disagreement. The general nature of the form permits flexibility of use regardless of the content and the process. The responses are collected, analyzed, and reported to provide feedback and improvement for future planning.

How do we select the right tool to process data? The next step to a successful survey is to treat survey responses as an asset of the district. This asset is one of the returns of investment (ROI) from putting in monetary, human, and time resources to organize the professional development day. In the light of ROI district officials must use the appropriate tools to store, manage, and analyze data.

Analyzing the survey responses using the Excel software requires many steps when the quantity of information input is large and the

Silverbrook School District

Professional Development Evaluation Form

Instructions: For each of the statements below, please circle your desired rating.
1 = Very Dissatisfied, 2 = Dissatisfied, 3 = Somewhat Dissatisfied, 4 = Fairly Satisfied,
5 = Satisfied, 6 = Very Satisfied.

Opening Session:

1. Keynoter's overall effectiveness	(1)	(2)	(3)	(4)	(5)	(6)
2. Content of the presentation	(1)	(2)	(3)	(4)	(5)	(6)
3. Presentation techniques	(1)	(2)	(3)	(4)	(5)	(6)
Session Rating	(1)	(2)	(3)	(4)	(5)	(6)

Comments:

_____

Breakout Session 1:

1. Presenter's overall effectiveness	(1)	(2)	(3)	(4)	(5)	(6)
2. Content of the presentation	(1)	(2)	(3)	(4)	(5)	(6)
3. Presentation techniques	(1)	(2)	(3)	(4)	(5)	(6)
4. Presentation materials	(1)	(2)	(3)	(4)	(5)	(6)
Session Rating	(1)	(2)	(3)	(4)	(5)	(6)

Comments:

_____

Breakout Session 2:

1. Presenter's overall effectiveness	(1)	(2)	(3)	(4)	(5)	(6)
2. Content of the presentation	(1)	(2)	(3)	(4)	(5)	(6)
3. Presentation techniques	(1)	(2)	(3)	(4)	(5)	(6)
4. Presentation materials	(1)	(2)	(3)	(4)	(5)	(6)
Session Rating	(1)	(2)	(3)	(4)	(5)	(6)

Comments:

_____

Thank you for completing the survey to help us improve!

Figure 3.5.   Professional Development Evaluation Form

quality is complicated. Unless the user is proficient in writing an Excel macro, following the steps can be a challenge. An option to the conventional data analysis method is the use of specialized statistical software. The specialized software usually has user-friendly graphical interface, vast selections of statistical methods, and presentation quality graphs and tables. A popular choice is the SPSS for Windows. This program is developed by the SPSS, Inc., of Chicago. You may want to visit the website www.spss.com for more information.

Let us begin with the data source prior to the data analysis. It is very common that the original data reside in an Excel file. There are good reasons to keep the data in an Excel spreadsheet. For example, a data entry clerk who may not have access to the SPSS software handles the survey responses, or data are pulled from a district Excel file depository. Regardless of the reasons, there is no need to store the original data in the SPSS file format simply because SPSS is capable of importing data from any Excel file in just a few simple steps.

Now, let us proceed to prepare the survey data for the Silverbrook School District Institute Day. The Institute Day has one opening session, two breakout sessions, and an exhibit session. The district received 286 completed forms from the participants and the response data are entered into an Excel spreadsheet (Figure 3.6).

	A	B	C	D	E	F	G	H	I	J	K	L	M	N
1	No.	Experience	Role	Location	Opening	A No.	A Relevance	A Quality	B No.	B Relevance	B Quality	Exhibits	Overall	
2	2	2	1		5	204	6					5	5	
3	3	4	1	1	4	49	6	6	23	4	3		4	
4	4	2	1	3	5	204	5	5	117	6	6	4	5	
5	5	1	1	3	6	117	6			6			6	
6	6	4	1		5	14	6	6	117	4	4		5	
7	7	4	1	3	3	95	6	6	128	6	5	3	4	
8	8	4	1	3	3	207	5	6	128	4	4	3	3	
9	9	4	1	3	4	103	5		122	5		3	3	
10	10	4	1	1	1	5	6	6	34	5	4	5	4	

Figure 3.6. Silverbrook Institute Day Data

The participants' satisfaction on the opening session, breakout session A, breakout session B, and the exhibit session are recorded in columns labeled *Opening, A Relevance, B Relevance,* and *Exhibits* respectively. The overall satisfaction on the institute day is in the last column labeled *Overall.* Satisfaction of the respondents is measured on a six-point scale: 1 = very dissatisfied, 2 = dissatisfied, 3 = somewhat dissatisfied, 4 = moderately satisfied, 5 = satisfied, 6 = very satisfied.

Furthermore, the spreadsheet also includes information about the participants' (1) years of experience in the district and (2) roles in the district. The years of experience are further classified into four categories: 1 = first year in district, 2 = 2 to 5 years, 3 = 6 to 10 years, and 4 = more than 10 years. Although the participants may have different work titles, they are nevertheless classified into two role categories: 1 = teaching staff and 2 = administrative staff.

With the above template prepared, we are ready to import this Excel spreadsheet data into SPSS. When SPSS is launched, a **What would you like to do?** welcome dialog will appear. Click the radio button for **Open an existing data source**. Then the **Open file** dialog will appear. SPSS has its own propriety data format. Files that are saved in this data format will usually have the file extension *sav*. To select the Excel file type: (1) go to the **Files of type**, (2) pull down its menu, and (3) select the **Excel (*.xls)** type. Navigate to the directory in which the *Silverbrook Institute Day.xls* resides. After you pressed the Open button, you should see the following **Open Excel Data Source** dialog.

Opening Excel Data Source   ✕

C:\USERS\BOOK\BOOK CHAPTERS\Silverbrook Institute Day.xls

☑ Read variable names from the first row of data.

Worksheet: A A&B B [A1:E136]   ⌄

Range:

Maximum width for string columns: 32767

| OK | Cancel | Help |

Since this Excel file contains more than one worksheet, you need to pull down the menu of **Worksheet** and select the Data Entry worksheet.

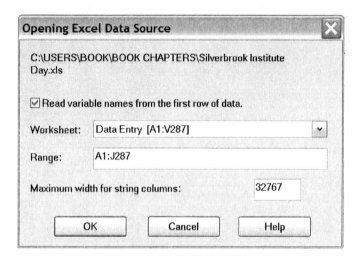

Leave the checkbox that labeled **Read variable names from the first row of data** checked because you want SPSS to use the column labels as variable names. Although the range shown in **Worksheet** field is A1:V287, you know that the data are all within the range A1:J287. Therefore, enter A1:J287 into the **Range** field. Now you can press the **OK** button. SPSS will now import the specified worksheet. You will see the resulting data next.

Before going further, it is always a good practice to save the data into an SPSS data file. The data is thereby stored as the *Institute Sessions 2001 Data Entry.sav*. You will notice that the variable names look different from the column labels in the Excel file. For example, the column label *A Relevance* becomes the variable name *ARelevance* because spaces are not allowed in a SPSS variable name. When you move the mouse pointer to the lower left corner and click on the **Variable View** tab, you will see the following:

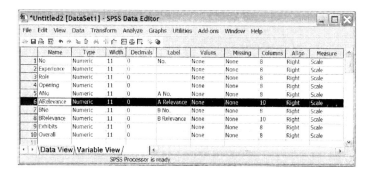

The variable *ARelevance* now has the label *A Relevance*.

Next, we want to label categories of *Experience* to make the output easier to read and ready for presentation. Here are the steps. First, move your mouse cursor to a cell in the **Values** column corresponding to the *Experience* variable.

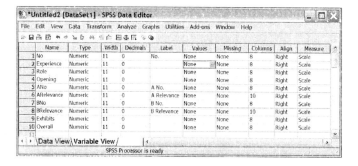

A button will now appear next to the cell content: **None**. Click on it to bring up the **Value Labels** dialog below. Next are the three steps to enter a label: (1) type the coded value of the category into the **Value**

field, (2) type the desired label into the **Value Label** field, and (3) click the **Add** button. For example, you will give value 1 of Experience the label *First year in district*. The dialog should look like the one below after you have completed the three steps. You can repeat these three steps to add another value label, or hit **OK** to exit from this dialog.

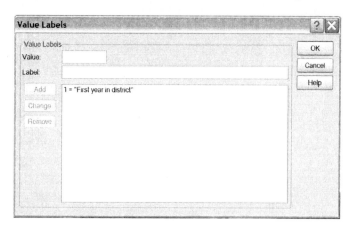

We continue to label all categories of *Experience, Role, Opening, ARelevance, BRelevance, Exhibits,* and *Overall*. The **Variable View** should now look similar to the screen below. To label all categories may be time consuming; however, the benefit is clear and easy-to-read output.

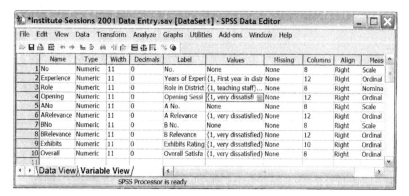

Summarizing the Data with Graphs

The first step many data analysts do is to make sure that they have the correct data for the task. Correct data mean getting accurate legitimate values in all variables and not finding variables with constant values or all missing values. A common way to inspect correct data is by looking at the frequency histogram chart. Follow the steps below to produce a graph.

Step 1: Pull down the **Graphs** menu and select the **Bar** option.

Step 2: You will now see the **Bar Charts** dialog box. Use the default options (**Simple** chart on **Summaries for Groups of Cases**). Click the **Define** button to proceed.

Step 3: You should now see the **Define Simple Bar: Summaries for Groups of Cases** dialog box. Suppose you want to generate a frequency bar chart for overall satisfaction, here are the steps: (1) highlight the variable *Overall*, (2) hit the arrow button (a triangle pointing to the right) to move this variable to the **Category Axis** field, and (3) click **OK** to complete the steps. The bar chart will now appear in the output window titled **Output1—SPSS Viewer**.

Figure 3.7 is a bar chart. It shows that most participants are either satisfied or moderately satisfied at the overall satisfaction level. How-

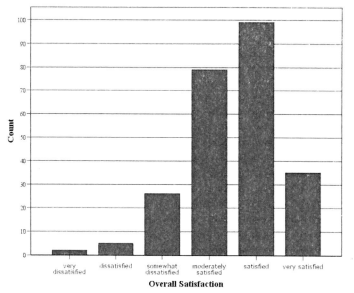

Figure 3.7.   Overall Satisfaction

ever, there are small but not negligible numbers of participants who are dissatisfied or very dissatisfied.

Although one can generally conclude that the Institute Day participants are satisfied with the programs, a meticulous data analyst will analyze the information further to find the variance of satisfaction levels between administrators and years of experience.

There are many ways to achieve this objective. Some rely on visual graphs, and others use quantitative statistical numbers. One of the visual methods to achieve the first goal is to redraw Figure 3.7 paneled by groups of participants. Participants are grouped according to their roles in the district and their years of experience. One can revisit the **Define Simple Bar: Summaries for Groups of Cases** dialog box and add these two as panel variables.

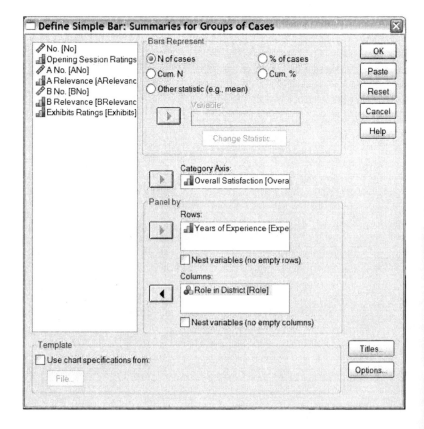

Upon clicking the OK button, you should see the output (Figure 3.8) in your Output Viewer window. It contains eight histograms (three are empty because no administrators or deans of students have less than ten years of experience).

One may notice that all teaching staff in their first year in the district are satisfied. Dissatisfaction starts to go up among the teaching staff as they have more experience. An interesting observation is that teaching staff having two to five years or more than ten years of experience are more open in expressing their opinions (both positive and negative).

Summarizing the Data with Numbers

Although the data analyst can get a quick view of the overall satisfaction levels, he or she may be hesitant to draw any conclusions until further quantitative evidence is found. A measure of central location is the first type of statistic that comes to the data analyst's mind.

A measure of central tendency describes the mass distribution of the data. Common measures of central tendency are mean, median, and mode. The mean is the arithmetic average of the satisfaction ratings. The median divides the participants into two equal-size groups.

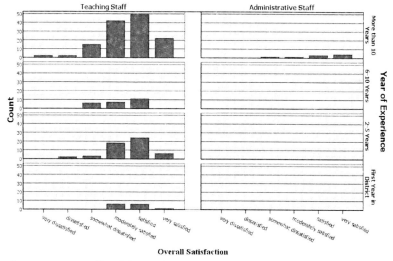

Figure 3.8.   Overall Satisfaction by Years of Experience and Roles in District

The median is less than or equal to the satisfaction ratings in one group, and greater than or equal to the satisfaction ratings in another group. A mode is the satisfaction rating with the highest frequency distribution. Since ties can occur, there can be more than one mode. When this happens, the mode with the lowest value is usually reported.

In the following example, we split the data jointly by years of experience and role in district. We can accomplish this task by choosing the **Data** menu, then the **Split File** item. Now you should see the **Split File** dialog box.

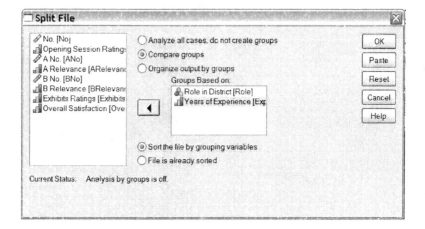

Select the **Compare Groups** radio button, then move Years of Experience and Role in District to the **Groups Based on:** target list. This specifies the two selected variables as the SPSS split file variables. SPSS for Windows requires data to be sorted in either ascending or descending order by the split file variables. Therefore, unless you are sure that your data are already sorted by Years of Experience and Role in District, we recommend that you select the **Sort the File by Grouping Variables** radio button. Finally, click **OK** to accept the specifications. Now you should see the text **Split File On** at the lower rightmost corner of the SPSS Data Editor (you may need to maximize the SPSS Data Editor window).

The mean, the median, and the mode are readily computed in many SPSS procedures. One handy choice is the Frequency procedure. To do that choose the **Analyze** menu, then the **Descriptive Statistics** menu, and finally the **Frequencies** item to obtain the mean, the median, and the mode. Move Overall Satisfaction into the **Variable(s):** list box. Click the **Statistics . . .** button to enter into the Frequencies: Statistics dialog box. Check the boxes next to **Mean, Median,** and **Mode** to request the desired statistics. Click **Continue** to return to the **Frequencies** dialog box. Finally, click **OK** to accept the specifications. The output tables are listed under the heading Frequencies in the Output View window.

SPSS produces professional output tables. SPSS also offers tools to rearrange (i.e. pivot) the table into a better presentable form. This SPSS output table is hence called pivot table. Suppose the data analyst wants to compute the mean, the median, and the mode to show in columns instead of in rows, the analyst will first activate the pivot table by double clicking it. Next, choose the **Pivot** menu, then the **Pivoting Trays** item. The Pivoting Trays will now appear in a small window shown below.

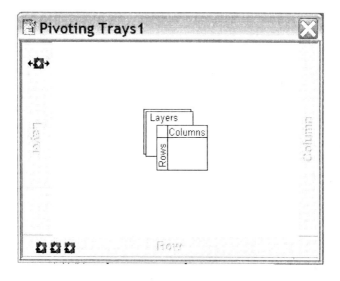

Each icon (a square with a diamond inside) on the dimension represents a particular type of information or a particular breakdown variable in the table. To find out what each icon represents, simply hover the mouse pointer over the icons. The rightmost icon on **Row** represents the statistics row dimension. Drag this icon from **Row** to

Column to display the statistics in columns. The pivot table is imme-
diately arranged. It should look like the following:

Statistics

Variables	Overall Satisfaction ⌄					

		N				
Role in District	Years of Experience	Valid	Missing	Mean	Median	Mode
.	.	0	1			
	First year in district	2	1	5.00	5.00	5
	2-5 years	2	0	3.50	3.50	3[a]
	6-10 years	1	0	2.00	2.00	2
	more than 10 years	8	1	4.63	4.50	4
teaching staff	.	2	1	5.50	5.50	5[a]
	First year in district	13	2	4.62	5.00	4[a]
	2-5 years	53	6	4.55	5.00	5
	6-10 years	24	5	4.21	4.00	5
	more than 10 years	132	22	4.52	5.00	5
administrative staff	more than 10 years	9	1	5.11	5.00	6

a. Multiple modes exist. The smallest value is shown

As you glance through this table, you will notice a period in Role
in District and a period in Years of Experience. This period is a symbol
used by SPSS to denote a system with missing value. In other words,
some participants did not enter their roles in district and their years
of experience on the evaluation forms due to oversight or a way to
avoid identification.

Since SPSS found zero valid cases when both Role in District and
Years of Experience are missing, the statistics cannot be computed
and therefore are displayed as system-missing values. We strongly
suggest the reinspection of data. There is only one case (Participant
no. = 215) when both Role in District and Years of Experience are
missing. This participant responded 1 (very dissatisfied) for the
Opening Session, 3 (dissatisfied) for the Breakout Session A, and 1
(very dissatisfied) for the Breakout Session B, and did not respond
to the Exhibit and the Overall satisfaction. A high level of dissatisfaction in this example is recorded and further investigation may be
warranted.

Missing values in surveys are very common, particularly those
administered to a large group of people. One can minimize missing
values by (1) avoiding ambiguity in writing the questions and (2) following up with participants (if possible) who did not respond. Missing values may mean loss of data, but more important, it may indicate
the presence of some undisclosed important information.

Planning Versus Evaluating Professional Development

What do the Silverbrook professional development evaluation data tell us? The participants, in general, indicated that the professional development experience is worthwhile and the institute day time well spent. The general initial satisfaction of the staff is a litmus test in the continuous professional development process. The satisfied professional development experience means that the staff is receptive to further development, further learning, and application. Unfortunately, if the reception is less than satisfactory, then further continuous training may face resistance.

What makes professional development effective? If it does not affect student learning the process should not be considered effective. A single professional development activity like an institute day can hardly address the issue of student learning outcomes. And this is why effective training activities are ongoing toward the goal of student success. Professor Thomas R. Guskey (2000) proposes a model for evaluating professional development. The model has five components and they are: (1) participants' reaction, (2) participants' learning, (3) organization support, (4) participants' use of new knowledge and skills, and (5) student learning outcomes. Participants' reaction measures the satisfaction of the professional experience. The participants' learning measures the new knowledge and skills learned by the participants. The organization support measures the organization's advocacy and support. The participants' use of new knowledge and skills measures the degree of implementation of the learning. Last, the student learning outcome measures the change in students' learning behavior. What is measured in each component of the model is progressive in complexity. More resources will be spent as we go from one level to the next to achieve student success. In planning a professional development activity (Figure 3.9) we start from the student learning outcomes and back map them to the use of knowledge and skill, to organization support and change, to learning from the experience, and to participant's reactions to the experience. On the other hand, when we evaluate a professional development activity we reverse the order and start with the participants' reactions to the experience. The example used in evaluating the professional development activities of Silverbrook School illustrates evaluation in its simplest and commonest form. The information is easy to collect and the experience familiar to many educators.

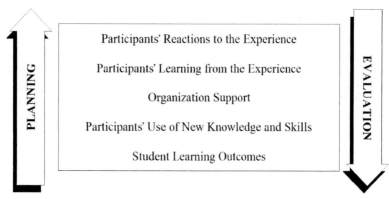

Figure 3.9. Planning and Evaluating Professional Development Activities

CHAPTER REFLECTION

1. Take the role of a teacher mentor. Explain to a nontenured teacher the purpose and process of walk-through supervision or coaching.
2. Explain how you would strategize your walk-through with a tenured teacher with twenty-five years of classroom experience. What are the dos and don'ts?
3. What would be your suggestions to a teacher showing a flat data trend in the walk-through data? How do you help this teacher to improve?
4. Create a Venn diagram to identify the similarities and differences between the skills of an *emerging* teacher and an *integrating* teacher.
5. Study the performance indicators of instruction. Describe the skill progression from an *applying* teacher to an *innovating* teacher referencing the performance description of *teaching interaction*.
6. What are the student placement procedures for the English Language Learner (ELL) program?
7. You are an ELL education consultant of a school district. Describe how you would prepare an ELL program evaluation report for the board of education.
8. Demonstrate how you can maneuver through Excel to generate

a pivot table to evaluate the performance of an instructional program such as ELL.

9. What are the basic considerations to evaluate a staff development program? How is evaluation different from planning a staff development program?

REFERENCES

Covey, Stephen. 1990. *The Seven Habits of Highly Effective People.* New York: Simon & Schuster.

Guskey, T. R. 2000. *Evaluating Professional Development.* Thousand Oaks, CA: Corwin Press.

Guskey, T. R., and Huberman, M. 1995. *Professional Development in Education: New Paradigms and Practices.* New York: Teachers College Press.

Marx, Gary. 2000. *Ten Trends: Educating Children for a Profoundly Different Future.* Arlington, VA: ERS Schools of the Future Council; Educational Research Service.

4

School District Community Improvement Accountability

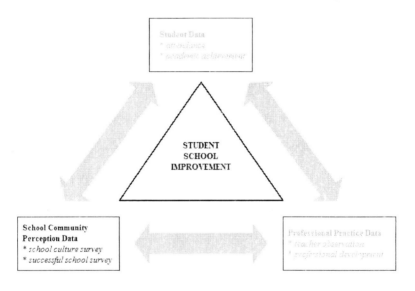

SCHOOL CULTURE STUDY

Public education in the 1980s came to focus on the importance of the workplace. The statement put forth for discussion is that the work environment influences the workers. In education, Rosenholtz (1989) and Darling-Hammond (1996) discussed how the work environment contributes to the productivity of the teachers. Needless to say, positive teacher productivity increases the intended student learning out-

comes. A major factor contributing to the work settings is the culture
of collaboration. Culture may be defined as all the practices, values,
and beliefs shared by a group or an organization. In the school, it is
characterized by staff working closely together to improve students in
a way that they would not be able to achieve independently. School
culture lies in the commonly held beliefs of teachers, students, and
principals. School culture shapes what people think and how they act.
In that sense, a healthy culture can be your friend, making things
work, or an unhealthy culture can deter things from working or students from learning—it is that powerful. Five factors (Huffman and
Hipp, 2003) contribute to making a school culture of collaboration:

1. Shared leadership
2. Shared vision
3. Shared learning
4. Shared personal practice
5. Supportive conditions

Shared school leadership goes beyond the office of the school
administrator. Transforming a school organization into a learning
community can be done with the school leaders and the encourage-
ment of the school staff's development as a community. Shared
school leadership takes courage because the administrator is perceived as a sharing and not an all-knowing leader. Sharing vision is
more than just listening to a good idea; it is a guidepost important to
all staff in a school organization. Staff are encouraged to get involved
in developing a shared vision and to use it to direct teaching and
learning in the school. Shared learning means teachers meeting and
sharing information about what they do. This shared learning can be
in the form of individual small groups or a large group. When learning is shared, teachers get together to reflect hypotheses, design action
steps, and arrive at common ground for improvement. Shared personal practice gives teachers the opportunity to visit and observe each
other to offer peer support on instructional practices. This way the
organization improves, the teachers improve, and more important,
the students also improve. Supportive conditions include physical
conditions, human qualities, and people capacities. One of the questions asked is, Do we provide time and place for people to collaborate
and reduce isolation? Time clearly is the resource to make collaboration happen. In building people capacity we might ask, Do we allow

people to trust each other, accept feedback, and work toward improvement? It is important to point out that the physical factor and the human factors are closely related to creating a school with supportive conditions.

Why is a culture of school collaboration (Hord) important for student and school improvement? Collaboration is about people working together on a common mission. A school may have a perfect improvement plan; however, if the foundation of collaboration is shaky then the goals of improvement will not be realized. Are you working in a professional learning community? How do you find out and how can your workplace improve? The Professional Learning Community (DuFour) survey is designed to measure the perceptions about the five factors contributing to the success of the school. The survey contains fifteen statements describing the factors and a scale to reflect the respondents' levels of agreement with the statement. The agreement scale can further be quantified by assigning numbers such as 1 = strongly disagree, 2 = disagree, 3 = agree, and 4 = strongly disagree.

Improved student achievement is the product of how well the people in a school work together. We can examine collaboration at three different levels—the teacher, the principal, and the district office. In a comparison study of successful and unsuccessful schools in California (Just and Boese, 2002) teachers were given the opportunity to:

1. Make decisions about teaching and learning
2. Meet as grade-level or subject-matter teams to discuss effective strategies
3. Develop peer leadership for teacher-initiated changes such as professional development to improve instruction

The same comparison study also shows some characteristics about the school administrator. The administrator needs to provide time for teachers to collaborate with structured support. The principal visits the grade-level or subject-matter team meeting regularly to seek feedback. The principal makes data-supported decisions to augment programs, interventions, and staff development. In a similar fashion, the district office is a key to improving low-performing schools. As one example, the district office provides adequate assessment data disaggregated by teachers and students. Again, the district office provides time for scheduled cohort meetings to share successes and challenges.

School Culture Survey

	1	2	3	4
(I) Shared Leadership				
Leadership is encouraged among school staff.	O	O	O	O
The school leader incorporates feedback from staff.	O	O	O	O
Responsibility and accountability are shared appropriately.	O	O	O	O
(II) Shared Vision				
Shared visions for school improvement drive decisions.	O	O	O	O
School staff are committed to enhance student learning.	O	O	O	O
Collegial relationships exist to promote student improvement.	O	O	O	O
(III) Shared Learning				
Staff share ideas for best practices in improving students.	O	O	O	O
There are opportunities for staff coaching and mentoring.	O	O	O	O
Staff training focuses on student improvement.	O	O	O	O
(IV) Shared Personal Practice				
Staff share ideas and results for improving students.	O	O	O	O
Staff are given the opportunity to visit and support peers.	O	O	O	O
Staff provide constructive feedback to peers about teaching.	O	O	O	O
(V) Supportive Conditions				
Staff relationships are built on trust and respect.	O	O	O	O
Achievement and success are celebrated in the school.	O	O	O	O
Time and place are provided for staff collaboration.	O	O	O	O

The encouraging picture that we have painted so far is that solutions to improving students do not need to go very far. They lie within the school district, the school, and the classrooms. Schools can bring about student achievement if they are willing to work collaboratively to examine what they do and change for improvement.

How do we change and improve school culture? If we believe that attitude is a building block of culture, then changing school culture is changing people's attitude. Attitude change is not the same as knowledge or skill change. It takes unrelenting time and effort. People who are interested in changing school culture should attempt first to understand the past and present culture. An understanding of that culture helps people to know a wide variety of relationships holding up the institutional stability. This stability factor explains why so many people are hesitant or resistant to cultural change. A group of school community representatives can get together and share their feelings about the positives and negatives of their school culture and identify the benefits from change. To move the school in the right direction for student improvement, shared leadership, shared vision, shared learning, shared practice, and supportive school conditions should be discussed, constructively criticized, and transformed into an action plan.

SUCCESSFUL SCHOOL STUDY

Educators are constantly interested to find out whether their schools have the ingredients of being successful (Wormeli). The case study on which we are going to embark is such an example. The Johnson Board of Education is eager to study the two middle schools (grades 6–8) due to declining student achievement and intensifying student discipline problems. The Office of Instruction was prompted to develop a study design aiming to survey the perception of the school community against the six characteristics of effective middle schools as described by the National Middle School Association. The purpose of the survey is to look at the strengths and the weaknesses against the characteristics, and to seek ways to improve. Four major steps are involved in the process: preparation, administration, analysis, and report of the survey. Schools interested in conducting an opinion survey of any sort can adapt the process to fit their study purpose. Figure 4.1 shows the four steps of the process.

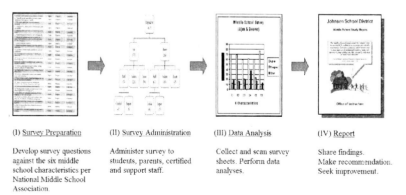

(I) Survey Preparation

Develop survey questions against the six middle school characteristics per National Middle School Association.

(II) Survey Administration

Administer survey to students, parents, certified and support staff.

(III) Data Analysis

Collect and scan survey sheets. Perform data analyses.

(IV) Report

Share findings. Make recommendation. Seek improvement.

Figure 4.1.   Four Steps of the Survey Process

Survey Preparation

The preparation of the survey questions is resource intensive. It is crucial that we write clear and accurate questions to find answers. The task of developing the questions is easier if one can align the items to a professional reference such as the characteristics of effective schools or the professional learning community. The six characteristics of effective middle school follow.

1. *Curriculum that is relevant, challenging, integrative, and exploratory.* An effective curriculum is based on criteria of high quality and includes learning activities that create opportunities for students to pose and answer questions that are important to them. Such a curriculum provides direction for what young adolescents should know and be able to do and helps them achieve the attitudes and behaviors needed for a full, productive, and satisfying life.

2. *Multiple learning and teaching approaches that respond to their diversity.* Since young adolescents learn best through engagement and interaction, learning strategies involve students in dialogue with teachers and with one another. Teaching approaches should enhance and accommodate the diverse skills, abilities, and prior knowledge of young adolescents, and draw on students' individual learning styles.

3. *Assessment and evaluation programs that promote quality learning.* Continuous, authentic, and appropriate assessment and evaluation measures provide evidence about every student's learning progress (McTighe). Assessment grades alone are inadequate expressions for assessing the many goals of middle-level education.

4. *Organizational structures that support meaningful relationships and learning.* The interdisciplinary team of two to four teachers working with a common group of students is the building block for a strong learning community with its sense of family, where students and teachers know one another well, feel safe and supported, and are encouraged to take intellectual risks.

5. *Schoolwide efforts and policies that foster health, wellness, and safety.* A school that fosters physical and psychological safety strives to build resiliency in young people by maintaining an environment in which peaceful and safe interactions are expected and supported by written policies, scheduled professional development, and student-focused activities.

6. *Multifaceted guidance and support services.* Developmentally responsive middle schools provide both teachers and specialized professionals who are readily available to offer the assistance many students need in negotiating their lives both in and out of school.

From the six middle school characteristics, twenty-five survey items were developed. These survey items were reviewed by a staff focus group led by the two middle school assistant principals. The survey questions were then refined and finalized to become the Johnson School District School Survey. The sequence of the twenty-five items was scrambled in the actual survey to avoid a specific questioning pattern. Respondents were asked to agree, to disagree, or to be undecided if they do not clearly understand the survey item. The twenty-five-item survey follows.

Characteristic 1: Curriculum is relevant, challenging and integrative, and exploratory.
1. Students receive a challenging academic education.
2. Reading, writing, and math are learned in all subject areas.
3. Exploratory classes prepare for real-world experiences.
4. Students experience a variety of reading, writing, and math projects in all subject areas.

Characteristic 2: Multiple learning and teaching approaches respond to the diversity of students.
5. Teachers use a variety of teaching techniques to meet the individual needs of students.
6. All staff accept that children learn at different rates and have different interests and backgrounds.
7. The staff have high expectations of every student regardless of race, gender, or ability level.
8. Assignments are relevant to what is being taught.
9. Technology is an important part of learning and instruction.

Characteristic 3: Assessment and evaluation programs promote quality learning.
10. Teachers in this school allow students to show what they know in different ways.

11. Assignments and tests provide students with feedback on how they can improve their learning.
12. Teachers effectively communicate learning goals to students.

Characteristic 4: Organizational structures support meaningful relationships and learning.

13. Parents and students are given assistance and support in the transition process from fifth to sixth, and eighth to ninth grades.
14. The school keeps me informed about what is going on in the building.
15. Teachers communicate to parents and students about student progress.
16. The house system promotes student learning.
17. The house system gives students a sense of belonging.

Characteristic 5: Schoolwide efforts and policies foster health, wellness, and safety.

18. School rules and standards of student conduct are consistently enforced.
19. The school has a strong sense of school spirit, pride, and tradition.
20. Students feel safe at school.
21. The physical environment provides a pleasant and welcoming place for students to learn.

Characteristic 6: Multifaceted guidance and support services.

22. Students feel connected to at least one caring adult.
23. Support is available if students need help with their schoolwork.
24. Support groups are available through guidance for students as needed.
25. Counselors are available to help solve problems students nay be having at school.

Survey Administration

The twenty-five-item survey was administered to all the eighth-grade students and parents (one per student household), and all certified and support staff in each middle school. Survey scan sheets were distributed to Ajax and Beaver. The returned survey scan sheets were divided into batches and scanned—Ajax student, Ajax support staff, Ajax certified staff, Beaver student, Beaver support staff, and Beaver certified staff. Obviously another option to machine scanning is to hand-enter the data if there is a small number of respondents. This pool of respondents is disaggregated into staff (certified and support), students, and parents. The organization chart below shows the categories and number of respondents.

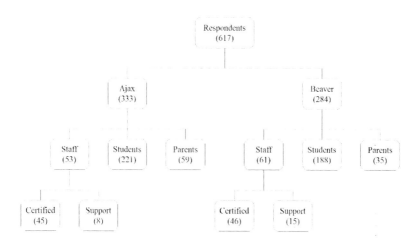

Survey Data Analysis

The scanner exports the results to a text file. From there, the text file results were converted into Excel and the batch flagged appropriately to identify the different respondent groups' answers. Lastly, the results were combined into a master Excel sheet. A snapshot of the master file is shown in the following:

School	Type	Q1	Q2	Q3	Q4	Q5	Q6	Q7	Q8	Q9	Q10
A	ST	1	2	1	1	3	1		2	1	
B	CS	1	2	2	2	2	1	2	2	1	2
A	ST	1	1	1	2	3	3	2	2	2	2
B	ST	1	2	2	1		3	2	1	3	3
A	SS	1	2	2	2	2	3	2	3	1	3
B	SS	1	1	3	1	3	1	1	3	2	3
A	ST	1		1	3	1	2	2	1	3	3
B	PT	1	2	3		3	2		2	3	3
A	ST	1	3	2	2	2	3	3	3	2	2
B	SS	1	1	1	3	3	1	3	1	3	1

Type key:
A = Ajax   B = Beaver
ST = Student   PT = Parent   SS = Support Staff   CS = Certified Staff

Cell value key:
1 = Agree   2 = Disagree   3 = Undecided   (blank) = Other

After overcoming the technical challenges in collecting, transmitting, and storing the information, the survey administrator next faces the challenge of finding messages that the data carry. This can be a daunting task for people with no or little training in analyzing survey data. Although there are many software programs (e.g., SPSS for Windows) that are developed to help make it easier to analyze survey data, the ultimate task of determining what questions to be answered still falls on the administrator's shoulder.

Now is a good time to revisit the purpose of conducting the survey: to study the strengths and the weaknesses against the characteristics, and to seek ways to improve. Before one can study the strengths and the weaknesses, one needs to find ways to measure the strengths and the weaknesses. A common measure is to count the number of 1s (Agree) in the questions that belong to a characteristic.

Let's use the first row of the above master file snapshot for illustration. A student in Ajax school answered 1 (Agree) to Q2 and Q4, and 2 (Disagree) to Q3, and this student did not answer Q1. Since Q1, Q2, Q3, and Q4 belong to the first characteristic, this student agrees to this characteristic. However, another student in Ajax (the ninth row in the snapshot) answered differently. That student answered 1 to Q1,

3 to Q2, and 2 to both Q3 and Q4, meaning that this student tends to disagree with this characteristic. If we go on to other rows in the master file, we are sure to be confused about the students' actual opinions. To make matters more complicated, the number of questions belonging to each characteristic is different. This calls for a better way to measure the strengths and the weaknesses, and for presenting the opinions in a cohesive matter.

Instead of the count of 1s, the administrator chose the percentage of 1s. This solved the problem of unequal number of questions in each characteristic. Instead of studying the individual rows of the data, the administrator chose to report the average percentage of agreement, the average percentage of disagreement, and the average percentage of others. The report presented on page 98 (Figure 4.5) will be disaggregated by school and by respondent's role (student, parent, support staff, and certified staff) in the survey.

Survey Report and Recommendations

Through the lenses of all the respondents, one can rank order the six characteristics of exemplary middle schools from the one with the most percentage of agreement to the one with the least percentage of agreement (Figure 4.2). The rank order of the six characteristics follows.

1. C6: Multifaceted guidance and support services
2. C1: Curriculum that is relevant, challenging, integrative, and exploratory
3. C2: Multiple learning and teaching approaches that respond to the diversity of students
4. C4: Organizational structures support meaningful relationships and learning
5. C5: Schoolwide efforts and policies foster health, wellness, and safety
6. C3: Assessment and evaluation programs promote quality learning

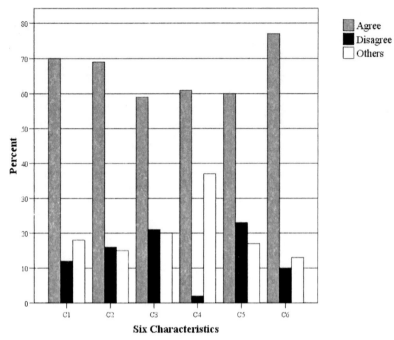

Figure 4.2. Middle School Survey: Ajax and Beaver

Through the lenses of all the Ajax respondents (Figure 4.3), one can rank order the six characteristics of exemplary middle schools from the one with the greatest percentage of agreement to the one with the lowest percentage of agreement. The rank order of the six characteristics follows. Note that there is a tie in the rank order of two characteristics.

1. C6: Multifaceted guidance and support services
2. C1: Curriculum that is relevant, challenging, integrative, and exploratory
3. C2: Multiple learning and teaching approaches that respond to the diversity of students
4. C4: Organizational structures support meaningful relationships and learning
5. C5: Schoolwide efforts and policies foster health, wellness, and safety
6. C3: Assessment and evaluation programs promote quality learning

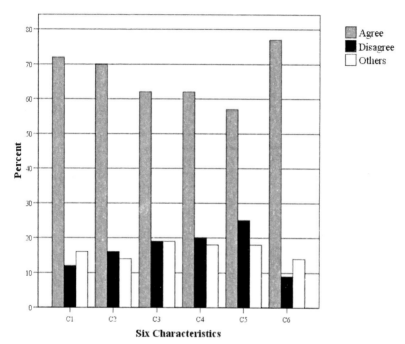

Figure 4.3. Middle School Survey: Ajax

Through the lenses of all the Beaver respondents (Figure 4.4), one can rank order the six characteristics of exemplary middle schools from the one with the greatest percentage of agreement to the one with the lowest percentage of agreement. The rank order of the six characteristics follows.

1. C6: Multifaceted guidance and support services
2. C1: Curriculum that is relevant, challenging, integrative, and exploratory
3. C2: Multiple learning and teaching approaches that respond to the diversity of students
4. C4: Organizational structures support meaningful relationships and learning
5. C5: Schoolwide efforts and policies foster health, wellness, and safety
6. C3: Assessment and evaluation programs promote quality learning

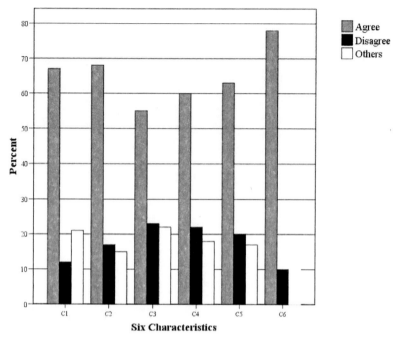

Figure 4.4.   Middle School Survey: Beaver

When the survey data are disaggregated by school, a variation of the rank order is evident. For example, the lowest ranked characteristics for the "Ajax all respondents" include schoolwide efforts and policies that foster health, wellness, and safety, while the lowest for "Beaver all respondents" is assessment and evaluation programs that promote quality learning. In general, the opinion profile of the respondent subgroups (i.e., students, parents, and staff, including administrators) mirrors the opinion profile of the school as a whole. One additional observation of the survey data is that among the three subgroups of respondents, the students are more critical than parents and staff. In other words, students tend to agree less than the other subgroups. On the other hand, staff members agree more on the six characteristics than the students and parents.

Here is a final remark. The administrator noticed that the numbers of Other for the C4 characteristic are consistently at the 30-percent level in the all respondents graph, and in individual school graphs.

This may suggest that the respondents are either refusing to answer the questions in the fourth characteristic or having difficulties in understanding the questions. Judging from the very low disagree percentage, the administrator has reason to believe the latter reason. Therefore, the administrator recommends rephrasing those questions in the next survey.

In the survey, reporting is a concluding section for making recommendations. Now that we know the strengths and weaknesses from the survey, what do we do with the information? Let us revisit Figure 4.2, the graph of the two middle schools, and identify the areas in need of most improvement. The two low areas in the bar graph indicate where the respondents had the least agreement. One area is characteristic 3 and the other is characteristic 5. Characteristic 3 deals with the assessment and evaluation programs that promote quality learning. Characteristic 5, on the other hand, deals with schoolwide efforts and policies that foster health, wellness, and safety. Let us examine the characteristics separately and suggest recommendations. Recommendations for improvement need to come from each middle school focus group and include staff, parents, and students. We may even include recommendations from high school students who attended Ajax or Beaver middle school.

Let us start the recommendation with characteristic 3. It is recommended that base information such as the fundamental principles of assessment and evaluation be given to facilitate the dialogue of the focus group participants about the subject. It is never effective when we invite people to discuss an issue and make recommendations without giving them the base information. The base information provides the participants with a common ground for discussion and interaction. The principles of assessment should include the purpose of promoting learning, the use of different sources of information, and the provision for valid, reliable, and fair information.

The first principle stresses the primary purpose of assessment is to improve learning and inform teaching. To achieve that purpose, the assessment process has to be continuous in lieu of a concluding activity at the end of instruction. When tests are given only at the end of a unit or chapter, students may feel that their learning needs are not sufficiently informed. Do you think this may be a cause for some survey respondents to disagree with characteristic 3? An item analysis based on the response of the respondents will verify that hypothesis. A second principle of assessment calls for the use of different sources

Figure 4.5. Survey Report Disaggregated by School and Respondent Role

	#1			#2			#3			#4			#5			#6		
	A	D	O	A	D	O	A	D	O	A	D	O	A	D	O	A	D	O
Ajax & Beaver	70	12	18	69	16	15	59	21	20	61	2	37	60	23	17	77	10	13
Ajax	72	12	16	70	16	14	62	19	19	62	20	18	57	25	18	77	9	14
Students	70	14	16	67	19	14	56	24	20	55	22	23	54	27	19	80	10	10
Parents	72	13	15	68	17	15	63	16	21	66	22	12	65	21	14	61	11	28
Certified Staff	83	4	13	91	2	7	94	0	6	90	4	6	60	22	18	89	2	9
Support Staff	50	14	36	69	2	29	52	7	41	67	18	15	50	25	25	81	6	13
Beaver	67	12	21	68	17	15	55	23	22	60	22	18	63	20	17	78	10	12
Students	60	15	25	60	22	18	45	31	24	49	28	23	55	26	19	74	13	13
Parents	71	10	19	66	13	21	59	20	21	64	21	15	71	16	13	71	13	16
Certified Staff	84	3	13	92	1	7	85	3	12	89	3	8	81	5	14	95	0	5
Support Staff	88	0	12	92	1	7	78	0	22	91	0	9	87	7	6	87	2	11

Keys:

#1: Curriculum that is relevant, challenging, integrative, and exploratory

#2: Multiple learning and teaching approaches that respond to the diversity of students

#3: Assessment and evaluation programs promote quality learning

#4: Organizational structures support meaningful relationships and learning

#5: School-wide efforts and policies foster health, wellness, and safety

#6: Multifaceted guidance and support services

A: Percent agree

D: Percent disagree

of assessment information. Applying this principle is important when the assessment information is used to make critical decisions such as promotion or report card grades. If the assessment practice is to place heavy weight on only one test, the student may call foul for not performing well on that particular test. Are the teachers at Ajax and Beaver taking frequent sampling of student learning using a variety of assessment methods? Ask the focus group participants to find out. The third principle of assessment concerns validity, reliability, and fairness. Validity deals with whether the test measures what it is supposed to measure. Asking test questions that are not related to instruction will be a violation of the validity rule. Reliability deals with the consistency of the assessment results. Under normal circumstances, the assessment results should reflect consistently what students should know and be able to do. Fairness deals with giving all students the opportunity to demonstrate what they have learned. A test that does not reflect what has been taught in the classroom is not a fair test.

Let us examine characteristic 5 dealing with health, wellness, and safety. The gist of characteristic 5 is based primarily on proper student management. The concern came initially from the Johnson Board of Education regarding an escalation of student discipline problems. The survey results are very good in pinpointing the same problem area objectively. How do we deal with student management effectively knowing that it is problematic? First and foremost we need to understand that management of students is best understood as a component of an instructional tool. The most effective student managers are those who understand the nature of the students and use what works, not what is penalizing. In other words, we do not poise to wait for the students to break the rules and give them the consequences. We need to look at student management as an embedded component of what we do in the classroom—teaching. As educators are we well planned to deliver a learning experience? This is proactive student management. As educators are we dealing with students appropriately? This is interactive student management. As educators how do we deal with students making bad decisions? This is reactive student management.

Proactive student management is what good teaching is about. An effective teacher prevents student management problems with a good lesson plan, one that is developmentally appropriate and cognitively engaging. A teacher who engages the students in meaningful learning is leaving little room for student displacement behaviors. To be proactive one needs to align the instruction with the young minds of the students so that the environment is conducive to learning. How do we deal or interact effectively with students? Are we treating students as equals, as subordinates, as friends, or as learners? How you treat students will impact on the effectiveness of what you ask them to do and what not to do. As teachers we need to play our role clearly. Do not confuse the students with being a friend one minute and a disciplinarian the next minute. A clear role of a teacher will give students a consistent message of what is expected of them. How do you deal with or react to an angry student? Do you allow the angry student to push your buttons and make the two of you explode? In defusing an exploding situation, base your decision on three rules. The first one is hopefully based on a school rule instead of your own impulsive judgment. The second rule is to be calm and avoid adding insult to injury. The third rule is to defuse the situation with humor and leave room for the student to save face. We have briefly discussed ways to manage students proactively, interactively, and reactively. As one teacher insightfully put it, "It's all about being an effective teacher to handle student management problems."

For the purpose of informing improvement, more and more schools are tapping the opinions of their constituents—students, parents, teachers, staff, administrators, and citizens—using opinion surveys. What we have seen thus far is the use of two traditional paper surveys. However, online surveys are getting popular. These clickable surveys are served up by companies or schools to get quick feedback. For one thing, the survey results are easier to prepare and tabulate, and they appear to get a higher response rate than the traditional paper surveys. Online surveys cover a broad spectrum of topics to include quality of the educational services, the student code of conduct, satisfaction with school programs, and families' plans for student enrollment. All in all, the online surveys address many customer service objectives. The survey results give schools a way to monitor how they are doing and how they can improve and do better. Online surveys, despite their ease to use, also have limitations. To begin with, some families still do not have Internet access. The rate of response can be poor if an online survey is not well advertised. Some schools go as far as holding prize drawings for respondents who complete the surveys. Online surveys can also have the unintended results of drawing respondents who are not wanted in the survey pool without the use of password protection. These undesirable respondents, unfortunately, can be politically inclined with a predetermined agenda to build a new school or to reduce taxes.

FORECASTING STUDENT SUCCESS: CORRELATION BETWEEN LOCAL AND STATE TEST DATA

Do you remember your preparation experience for a high-stakes examination such as the American College Testing (ACT) for college entrance or the Graduate Record Examination (GRE) for graduate school admission? As part of the preparation, some students practice simulated test questions to get a feel of what the real test is like. These virtual test questions are not the real test; however, they have a certain relationship with the actual test questions. If there is a tight relationship between the practice tests and the actual test, one can predict the level of achievement success. There are test preparation companies that can forecast student test success just by estimating the relationship between the achievement of the practice test and the real test. In statistics such an estimation is called a correlation study.

Let us review the concept of correlation before continuing to discuss how correlation can help us to forecast student success. Correlation measures the degree that two quantitative variables are linearly related. The Pearson correlation coefficient is widely used by statisticians to study the correlation between two quantitative variables. This correlation coefficient is expressed between negative one (-1) and positive one ($+1$) inclusively. The strength of relationship between two variables increases as the correlation coefficient moves in both directions from zero. The strength reaches its maximum when the correlation coefficient is either $+1$ or -1. A correlation coefficient of $+1$ designates a perfect correlation where a variable changes at the same rate as the other variable. A correlation coefficient of -1 also designates a perfect correlation but the variables change in the opposite direction. Perfect correlations are essentially never found in the social sciences and exist only in mathematical formulas and direct physical or numerical relations. An example of a perfect correlation would be the relationship between the number of hours worked and the wages received by hourly paid workers. As the variable *hour* increases, the other variable *wage* will also increases at the same rate. Conversely, as *hour* decreases, *wage* will also decreases at the same rate. Another example of perfect correlation of $+1$ is when a variable is correlated with itself, or the two variables are identical copies of each other. How about a correlation of zero? Zero correlation means a nonlinear relation between two quantitative variables. For example, we would not expect IQ and height in inches to be correlated. We need to emphasize that two totally independent variables will have zero correlation, but the converse does not necessarily hold. Let us look at an example. Suppose values of the first variable are consecutive integers from -10 to $+10$, and values of the second variable are squares of the first one. The correlation coefficient between this variable and its square is zero even though the second variable totally depends on the first one!

Correlation measures the degree of linear relationship between two variables, but it does not explain *how* the two variables are related. Correlation does not necessarily explain causation. Often a strong correlation between two variables is due to a causal relationship with a third variable. Let us use the hourly paid workers example again to illustrate the point. Wages and work-related accidents may be correlated, but one would hesitate to conclude that the frequency of accidents at work can lead to higher wage. In fact, both variables are caused by the third variable—number of hours worked. The worker who works long hours will earn more wages but experience more fatigue. It is a known fact that fatigue is a primary contributing factor to frequency of work-related accidents.

Now let us return to see how correlation can help us to forecast student success. Many school districts use local student assessment to prepare students for the high-stakes state examination. Local assessments have the benefit of being administered to the students more frequently than the less frequent once a year state examination. For that reason, the local test data can be used to prepare the students for the state test by helping the teachers to adjust their instruction for better student achievement outcomes.

The Johnson School District had recently piloted High Score, a computerized assessment system. High Score claimed that using its test data, schools can better predict and therefore prepare students for the high-stakes state test. The Johnson Board of Education was skeptical about the High Score claim and requested a verification study. The question asked was, "What is the predictability of High Score with reference to the students' state test success?" The district's office of accountability designed a correlation study to verify the High Score claim. In this correlation study two variables were analyzed. High

Score test scores and state test scores in reading, language, and mathematics were compared in a sample of 452 fourth-grade students and 486 eighth-grade students.

The correlation coefficient is a value that measures the degree of association between two variables. It is readily computed in the SPSS correlation procedure. To conduct an SPSS correlation study, first choose the **Analyze** menu, then the **Correlate** menu, finally the **Bivariate . . .** item to invoke the correlation procedure. Select the variables whose correlation coefficients have to be computed, and move the selected variables into the **Variable(s):** list box. SPSS offers three types of correlation coefficients but the Pearson correlation coefficient is the most widely used type. Select the variables whose correlation coefficients are computed into the **Variables** box. Select the Pearson correlation coefficient. Finally, click **OK** to accept the specifications. The output tables are listed under the heading *Correlations* in the Output View window. The table below shows the SPSS output that contains the Pearson correlation coefficients between reading High Score and reading state test score of first year fourth grade. The Pearson correlation coefficient is 0.780 between these two variables.

Correlations

		Reading High Score of First Year Fourth Grade	Reading State Test Score of First Year Fourth Grade
Reading High Score of First Year Fourth Grade	Pearson Correlation	1	.780*
	Sig. (2-tailed)		.000
	N	452	452
Reading State Test Score of First Year Fourth Grade	Pearson Correlation	.780*	1
	Sig. (2-tailed)	.000	
	N	452	452

**. Correlation is significant at the 0.01 level (2-tailed).

The SPSS correlations procedure always tests whether the Pearson correlation coefficient is zero or not. The statistical significance of this test is displayed as *Sig. (2-tailed)*. The value .000 indicates that the correlation 0.780 is significantly non-zero (as indicated by the double asterisks). In fact, it indicates a fairly strong relationship between the reading High Score and the reading state test score.

Our goal is to forecast the reading state test score using the reading High Score; however, we may also explore the causality effect. A correlation of 0.78 means when the Reading High Score increases one standard deviation (of reading high score), the reading state test score will, on the average, increases 0.78 standard deviation (of reading state test score) respectively. Now suppose standard deviations of the reading High Score and the reading state test score are five and ten points respectively. The correlation of 0.78 means when the reading High Score increases 5 points (1 standard deviation of reading high score), the reading state test score will, on average, increase 7.8 points (0.78 standard deviation of reading state test score). Furthermore, suppose the district has set a goal to improve reading performance on the state test. In order to achieve this goal, students' state test score must move up sixteen points on average. This in turn requires students' High Score test score to move up ten points on average. Since the High Score test can be administered several times during a school year, the district can use the High Score test to calibrate the likelihood of meeting the student achievement goal.

The correlations of the local assessment and the state test in reading, language, and mathematics in the Johnson School District were compared for two consecutive years. The correlation comparison is shown in the table below.

High Score State Test Correlation Comparison

	Reading		Language		Mathematics	
	Year 1	Year 2	Year 1	Year 2	Year 1	Year 2
Grade 4	0.78	0.75	0.76	0.75	0.82	0.81
Grade 8	0.76	0.77	0.77	0.76	0.87	0.85

It is evident from the results that the correlations across the board are high (with respect to most educational researches) and the results are consistent for two consecutive years in all three subjects. One can conclude that (1) the High Score test emulates the state test and (2) students' performance on the High Score test accurately forecasts their performance in the state test. The High Score testing program is, therefore, a useful tool for improvement because it better prepares students for the high-stakes state test. In addition, the high correlation allows teachers to better focus their task from teaching to learning, a premise of a professional learning community.

CHAPTER REFLECTION

1. Describe the culture of your classroom. How is the culture of your classroom similar to and different from the culture of the school? Please explain.

2. How are the five factors of culture related to the seven correlates of effective schools?
3. Design a study to survey the culture of a high school classroom.
4. How do you bring about significant changes in the culture of an organization?
5. Describe a solution to compromise the conflicting opinions of parents and teachers in a school survey.
6. How is good teaching related to effective student management?

REFERENCES

Darling-Hammonds, L. 1996. "The Quiet Revolution: Rethinking Teacher Development." *Educational Leadership* 53 (6): 4–10.

Dufour, Richard, and Eaker, Robert. 1998. *Professional Learning Communities at Work: Best Practices for Enhancing Student Achievement.* Bloomington, IN: National Educational Service.

Hord, S. M. 1997. *Professional Learning Communities: Communities of Continuous Inquiry and Improvement.* Austin, TX: Southwest Educational Development Laboratory.

Huffman, J. B., and Hipp, K. K. 2003. *Reculturing Schools as Professional Learning Communities.* Lanham, MD: Scarecrow Education.

Just, A. E., and Boese, L. E. 2002. *Immediate Intervention/Underperforming Schools Program: How California's Low-Performing Schools Are Continuing Their Efforts to Improve Student Achievement.* Sacramento: California Department of Education Policy and Evaluation Unit.

McTighe, J., and Ferrara, S. 1994. *Assessing Learning in the Classroom.* Washington, DC: National Education Association

Rosenholtz, S. J. 1989. *Teachers' Workplace: The Social Organization of Schools.* New York: Longman.

Wormeli, R. 2003. *Day One and Beyond.* Portland, ME: Stenhouse.

5

Putting It All Together in the Continuous School Improvement Plan

SCHOOL IMPROVEMENT RESEARCH

We traced two decades of educational reform in the first chapter leading to the use of data and the regulation of school accountability. In the final chapter we go full circle to revisit another historical account of education reform in the professional learning community and effective schools. This account of school improvement is the purpose of using data and imposing school accountability.

Student achievement has been a discussion topic in education and researchers have been coming up with ways to achieve it. In 1966, J. S. Coleman, then a professor at Johns Hopkins University, and his research team came up with a report claiming that they had found the factors hampering students from learning well. The Coleman report concluded that the family factors and not the school factors were the major determinant of student achievement. Family factors can be the family earning, the education level of the parents, and so on. The influence of the family factors on learning was so strong that the report implied that methods of instruction would make little difference. The report painted a grim picture of learning for poor students. Starting in the 1970s, attention was given to the effective school research and its relationship to the school improvement process. Ron

Edmonds, then a Harvard University professor, came around and provided research to show that all children can learn and that the school controls the factors necessary to ensure student learning of the core curriculum. The family and school factors are exclusive of each other in influencing the achievement of students. While schools may be primarily responsible for students to function adequately in the school, the family is also responsible in determining how hard the students strive in the school. In conducting the effective schools research, Edmonds concluded that there are certain characteristics common to high-poverty, high-performance schools: strong instructional leadership, a strong sense of mission, demonstrated effective instructional behaviors, high expectations for all students, frequent monitoring of student achievement, and a safe and orderly school environment. These attributes eventually became known as the correlates of effective schools (Edmonds). Over the years, the correlates have been further developed into the following:

1. Instructional leadership
2. Clear and focused mission
3. Safe and orderly environment
4. Climate of high expectations
5. Frequent monitoring of student progress
6. Positive home–school relations
7. Opportunity to learn and student time on task

In the effective school, the principal is the primary person for providing instructional leadership. The principal understands and applies instructional effectiveness in the supervision of the school program. The principal makes sure that all the stakeholders have a shared sense of purpose and the mission of the organization. The principal as a strong instructional leader is a prerequisite of but not the isolated contributor to an effective school. In the effective school, there is a clearly stated mission that the school community shares an understanding. This notion of a shared sense of mission is one way to ascertain that the whole school is moving forward in one direction. In the effective school the school climate is conducive to teaching and learning. We want schools to be safe because the presence of a safe learning environment enhances learning. A safe school environment must have rules and consequences. Rules are to be firm and enforced with fairness and consistency by all school staff and administrators in the school. Unfair and inconsistent practice will undermine and destroy the orderly environment of a school.

In the effective school, there is a high-expectations atmosphere in which the staff believe and demonstrate that all students can learn. They also believe that they, the staff, have the capability to help all students obtain that mastery. An expectation is the internal belief that the adults have that the students can and will meet those high standards of learning. In the effective school, student progress is measured frequently, to improve student behaviors and performances. How often should a teacher monitor student progress? The answer depends on how often the teacher is prepared to use the assessment information to adjust or improve instruction. In the effective school, parents support the mission of the school and are given opportunities to help the school to reach its mission. Look at the participation of parents in an after-school student activity or a parent–teacher conference. Parent attendance usually is a good indicator of parent support unless some of the parents have to work the second shift or reside far from the school. In the effective school, the teaching staff use a significant amount of classroom time to teach in the core curricular areas. For a high percentage of this time, students are engaged in active learning. Students tend to learn what they spend time on. When the teacher is clear on what students should be learning, students should be given the time to learn it.

Putting all the effective school correlates together, a key concept of student success can be expressed simply in the following:

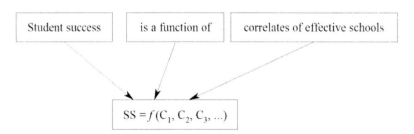

The above representation is pivotal to student improvement. What it means is that the output of student success is a direct function of the effective school correlates that go into it. To change the student success output, we must identify and understand the nature and the influence of the input variables. We need to increase the input (i.e., effective school correlates) to increase the student success output.

Let us pause for one moment to reflect on the connection between the effective school correlates and our early discussion on using data to improve students and schools. How do we connect the two? It is clear that the correlates are the goals to be achieved and the data are the indicators of progress and success. The figure below shows how the effective school correlates and the indicators are connected.

Correlates of Effective Schools
1. Instructional leadership
2. Clear and focused mission
3. Safe and orderly environment
4. Climate of high expectations
5. Frequent monitoring of student progress
6. Positive home–school relations
7. Opportunity to learn and student time on task

Indicators of Success
1. Student data
2. Professional practice data
3. School community perception data

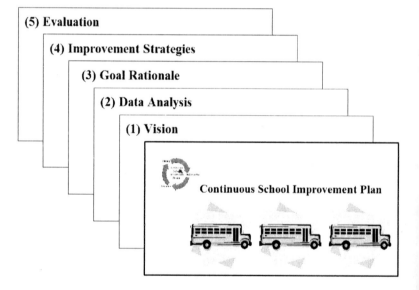

Under the No Child Left Behind (NCLB) law many schools are coming together to develop a plan to guide their improvement efforts. The improvement template that we are going to discuss has five components: (1) vision, (2) data analysis and interpretation, (3) goal rationale, (4) improvement strategies, and (5) evaluation. One way to organize the five components is to place them under three broad questions.

(I) Where are we now?
    a. Data analysis (need assessment)
(II) Where do we want to go?
    a. Vision
    b. Goal rationale
    c. Improvement strategies
(III) How do we know when we get there?
    a. Evaluation

Following is a description and discussion of each of the five components in the school improvement plan template.

The Vision

What is school vision? A vision is a statement of focus; it gives direction to the school. The school vision aligns with the school district's vision for improvement. Let us examine the vision statement from three schools and make a comparison.

Abraham Elementary School:

Our vision is to educate all students to their fullest potential and provide a nurturing environment which builds self esteem, through a process of shared decision making between students, staff, family, and community. This is accomplished within a climate of continuous improvement and respect for the diversity of others.

Beatrice Middle School:

Our vision is to help all students to be successful, achieve their highest potential, and set measurable goals to improve their learning. For students to reach their highest potential, our purpose is to educate all students in a caring, and understanding climate which reflects human dignity and respect through partnership of students, parents and community. We will provide opportunities for our students by differentiating the way we address individual learning styles.

Coleman High School:

Our vision, through a shared commitment by students, parents, staff and community is to provide [a] quality learning opportunity in a just and caring climate that promote[s] high expectations for educational

Chapter 5

and personal growth, recognize[s] individual worth and creativity, encourage[s] each student to become a self-sufficient, contributing member of the society.

What is the common denominator for the three school vision statements? Are there reasons to believe that the three schools are from different school districts or from the same school district and why? A characteristic of a vision is that the statement is very general, difficult to measure, and finally it represents a destination that still has to be reached. School improvement is impossible to accomplish if the destination is too general and difficult to measure. Such statement as "educate all students to their fullest potential" or "help all students to be successful" should have further suggestions regarding what areas to improve and how to do it. Despite its generality, a vision is important to define the framework for school improvement. One might conclude from the previous three vision statements that the framework is the improvement of students through a collaboration of the stakeholders in the school community.

Data Analysis and Interpretation

In order to support the vision of a school or a school district we need to study bundles of student and school data. The information answers the question, Where are we now? in the form of a needs assessment. In the previous chapters we discussed the different data sources as student, professional practice, and school community perception. After a careful review of the data the school needs to determine the area of strengths and weaknesses and develop goals for improvement. Let us review a high school data analysis report and follow that with the rationale for developing the improvement goals.

The entire school staff analyzed the results from the state and local tests. After the analysis, the following conclusions were reached: (a) Last year's state test data did not show any areas of real concern. (b) Our students scored noticeable increases in the proficiency levels in all subject areas (i.e. reading, English language arts, mathematics, science, and social studies) as measured by the state test. (3) The percentage of special education students failing to move up to the proficient and advanced areas in reading remains a concern. (4) Although the economically disadvantaged students improved noticeably in reading and mathematics, the scores still lag behind the non–economically disadvantaged students. The proficiency level in reading increased from 58% to 69%. (5) The

ACT scores continued to demonstrate improvement for all students. The composite score for all students increased from 22.5 to 23.1. Students who took core (i.e. college prep) curriculum significantly exceed the core state average in all subject areas by an average of 0.8. (6) The current graduation rate of 96% exceeded the state average of 82%.

Goal Rationale

We need to set improvement goals that are reasonable within the availability of the time and the resources. Setting too many goals for improvement might mean completing none. The approach to tackle a broad goal in order to get big improvement is usually ineffective. It is much more practical to focus on a specific component of a goal/problem. The main objective is to narrow the goal so that you can use your time and resources most effectively. In other words, we need to prioritize. Graphical displays can help us structure and prioritize goals in order to find relationships that will shed light on the problem area. We can use a fishbone diagram to get the goals prioritized.

Figure 5.1 illustrates the different components of a goal. The fishbone layout shows the relationship between the goal and the subgoals (1, 2, 3). The arrows lead from the subgoals to the "backbone" and then to the "head" or the major goal in discussion are the strategies supporting the goals. In doing a fishbone diagram it is important to note that the relationship (i.e., the arrow) must be verified with data for confirmation. As we go from the shaded box (the goal) on the right to the white boxes (subgoals), the targets for improvement go from broad and general to narrow and specific. As you move from

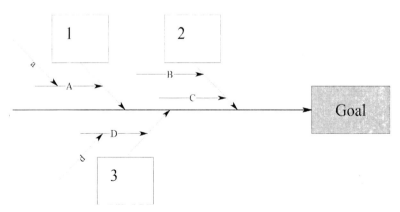

Figure 5.1.   Fishbone Diagram of Prioritization

right to left, you proceed from the improvement goal to more specific reasons making up the goal. Let us practice using a fishbone diagram. Let us assume that the main target of improvement based on test data is mathematics. The improvement of mathematics than becomes the main goal of improvement. It is the head of the fish. Further test data disaggregation shows that there are three weak student subgroups and they are special needs students, English language learner (ELL) students, and free lunch students. The three student subgroups are the subgoals of improvement. Further data analysis identified the teachers as the main factor common to impacting the achievement of the three student subgroups. Contributing to the deficiency of the special needs teacher and teachers with free lunch students is their effectiveness in teaching different-learning-style students. One other factor contributing to the less than satisfactory performance of the ELL student is textbook shortage. Figure 5.2 illustrates the fishbone diagram application.

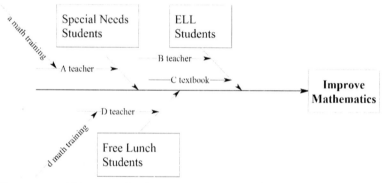

Figure 5.2.   Fishbone Application Diagram

The following goal statement is based on the information from the fishbone application diagram.

Our school met the annual yearly progress (AYP) in test participation, reading, and graduation rate; nevertheless, the school did not make the 4th grade mathematics AYP this year. We choose to continue the goals for improving student's mathematics across the curriculum. Special emphasis will be on the ELL students, the special education and economically disadvantaged students in our desire to narrow the achievement gaps. We will heighten our math training for teachers teaching special need students and low social economic status students. We want to make sure that the math textbook for the ELL program is instructionally appropriate and in no short supply.

Goals for improvement are developed based on the priority needs interpreted from the data analysis. Ask the following questions after writing the goals for improvement. Is it Specific? Is it Measurable? Is it Attainable? Is it Relevant? Is it Time dependent? Including all the characteristics in the statement will make a goal SMART. A SMART goal formula (Sargent) follows:

> The school will [action verb] [object] so that [which and how many students] [will demonstrate] [level of quality] [performance or behavior] as evidenced by measurement device [by when].

How is the following goal statement aligned to the SMART goal formula? Can you write variations to reflect the SMART formula?

> All grade 4, 8, and 10 students will achieve in reading and mathematics as measured by the Wisconsin Knowledge and Concepts Examination (WKCE) so that the school will meet and exceed the yearly progress goals.

Improvement Strategies

The school improvement team will spend quite a bit of time in developing the improvement strategies to answer the questions, Where do we want to go? and How do we get there? There are seven subtopics under the improvement strategies: (1) goal statement, (2) objectives, (3) action steps, (4) indicators of success, (5) time line, (6) necessary support, and (7) person/people responsible. Putting all the subtopics together will make an improvement strategies page similar to the template on page 116. On page 117 is a sample improvement strategies page addressing the improvement of mathematics in an elementary school. For each improvement strategy we need to assess the potential success against a set of criteria. Some common criteria are:

1. What are the potential benefits to student success? (Refer to the fishbone diagram.)
2. Which subgoals are tackled? (Refer to the fishbone diagram.)
3. Which improvement strategies are addressed? (Refer to the fishbone diagram.)
4. How easy will this be to implement?
5. What are the potential barriers to success?
6. What is the cost?

Not all criteria are equally important, so you need to decide which are the most important for your improvement plan. One approach for developing weighed criteria is to have the school improvement team vote on them.

School Improvement Strategies

Goal Statement: (SMART)					
Objectives	Action Steps	Indicators of Success	Timeline	Necessary Support	People Responsible
(1)					
(2)					
(3)					

Attach data to document your indicators of success.

Submitted by: _____   Date: _____

☐   Reviewed by Assistant Superintendent of Curriculum & Instruction   Date: _____

☐   Reviewed by Superintendent   Date: _____

☐   Approved by the Board of Education   Date: _____

Goal statement: (SMART): Improve schoolwide student achievement in mathematics leading to 86-percent proficient and advanced as measured by the state annual examination. In addition, the school will work toward local assessment growth to reflect the following scores in the spring in math: 2nd grade = 194.7; 3rd grade = 208.3; 4th grade = 212.7; 5th grade = 223.2.

Objectives	Action Steps	of Success	Timeline	Resource	Responsible
Students will be able to think flexibly when computing numbers	Use Math Challenger to accelerate our top learners	Ongoing classroom formative assessment	Classroom formative assessment is monthly	Quarterly staff development in the effective use of the Math Success program	The K-5 teaching staff as the implementer of the Math Success program
	Use a variety of strategies to explain methodologies	Common K-5 unit assessment	Common unit assessment is by semester	Monthly release time for staff to meet to discuss successes and challenges	Principal as the instructional head coach for Math Success
	Use whole numbers, fraction, decimals at the appropriate level of instruction per the district's learning continuum guide	Final results from the state test	The state test is given in the spring of the year	Additional acquisition of math manipulatives for every classroom	The math lead teachers as the assistant coaches, for the effective application of strategies
	Use flexible grouping and team teaching with special education staff				The IT director as the researchers for data collection, analysis and interpretation

Evaluation

Now that we have the goals and the strategies in place, how do we know when we get there? Similar to many educational processes, we need to check the successful completion of the goals, a method we call evaluation. When doing an evaluation, we are looking for evidence of completion or success. These evidences will differ as we go from planning to implementation to evaluation. The following template illustrates how an evaluation checklist might look in tabular form. The evaluator can easily complete the checklist and add comments as needed. It is possible that the information from the evaluation report can feed fresh information for the planning of a new school improvement plan for the following year; thus, the effort is continuous and sustained.

School: _____ Date: _____

The School Improvement Process	There is evidence of: (check all that apply)	Comments:
PLANNING	____ School improvement team training	
	____ School vision statement	
	____ Data collection	
	____ Data analysis	
	____ Data interpretation	
	____ Data-driven goals	
IMPLEMENTATION	____ Action plans are implemented	
	____ Staff development is a part of the plan	
	____ Formative assessments are documented and used for improvement	
EVALUATION	____ The improvement plan has resulted in improved student achievement	
	____ There is documented evidence of improved student achievement	
	____ There is little evidence of improved student achievement; there is evidence of further data analysis and plans for improvement	

Reviewed By: _____ Date: _____

At this stage of the evaluation process, follow through on the plans to check by collecting and analyzing new data, determining whether sufficient improvement has been made, and evaluating how well the school improvement is followed. A school is ready to move to standardization only if there are satisfactory results and you know how you got them. Standardization is replicating a successful process to sustain the effort. The following chart can be used to guide the standardization decision.

		Did you get satisfactory results?	
		Yes	**No**
Did you follow the plan?	**Yes**	*You did what you planned to do and got the results you wanted.*	*You did what you planned to do but did not get the results you wanted.*
		Go to standardization.	Return to data analysis and reset goals. Study the discrepancy. Collect more data.
	No	*You got the results you wanted despite not doing what you planned to do.*	*You didn't do what you planned and got poor results.*
		Decide the causes of the results —what did you accidentally do right? Understand how you achieve good results then go to standardization.	Go back to data analysis. Would your initial plans solve the problem? Try again with initial plans or revise as needed.

COMMUNICATION WITH THE SCHOOL COMMUNITY

If you as a teacher want support from the parents, do you not have to communicate with them about the students? As a principal if you want support from the parent–teacher organization (PTO), do you not have to communicate with the PTO about the school? As a district administrator if you want support from the community, do you not have to communicate with the citizens about the school district? Communication with the school community has a business function of building relationships and seeking support from its constituents

(Dembski). The base premise of communication is that it is an inter-active two-way process. For example, the school may present informa-tion to the public and at the same time invite the public to respond in school board meetings, committee meetings, and informal feedback surveys.

How do we deal with communicating the good news and the bad news? It is always easy when you have a good school or student story to share; you simply tell as it is. How about bad news? Well, that still has to be communicated. In times of negative publicity we still have to be honest and accurate with the key message. Let us look at how a school is telling the school community about how students failed to meet the AYP through a board meeting presentation and a parent newsletter.

> This year the school did not make the adequate yearly progress with our English language learner students. Of the 112 students in this group, we tested 95%. Of these, 25% of the students have cognitive disabilities, and 10% have learning disabilities. Our English as a Second Language, special education staff, and regular education teachers work with these students daily to maximize their learning. However, it is an extreme challenge for some students, especially those with language difficulty and cognitive disabilities, to meet the state proficiency standards. Based on the students' progress from year to year, we can assure you that these students are learning and mastering life skills that will enable them to function successfully in our community.

The AYP presentation shows us a number of fundamentals of all effective communication efforts. First, the board presentation is hon-est and accurate. After delivering the key message of not meeting the AYP the presentation goes on to give more details. These details include the composition and characteristics of the students. The com-munication finishes on a positive note regarding the ongoing efforts and an assurance of hope for success. Please note the difference between *not meeting* and *failing* the AYP. The original NCLB documen-tation uses the words *not meeting*, not *failing*. Second, in the sample parent letter, the key message is again factual. It gives a brief account of the historical development of the NCLB law and its components affecting school transfer and supplemental student services. Again, the communication finishes with a firm school commitment and a request for support.

Parents and citizens react to the bad news of not meeting the AYP

SAMPLE LETTER

Dear Parent/Guardian:

SCHOOL NAME is committed to provide all students with the educational opportunity to make them successful. We have set rigorous academic standards to ensure your child's success. While setting high standards is not new, the way our school and student achievement is measured and reported will be different under the No Child Left Behind (NCLB) law.

NCLB was signed into law in 2002. Two important components of the law include provision of school choice and supplemental education services for students attending schools that have been identified as needing improvement for not making the Adequate Yearly Progress (AYP) for two or more years in a row. AYP is based on student performance results on the STATE TEST. SCHOOL NAME has been identified as needing improvement.

Under NCLB, students at SCHOOL NAME may apply for transfer to designated schools in the school district that have made the AYP. If your child is eligible and you choose to exercise the option of transfer, the school district has the obligations to provide transportation to the new school.

Under NCLB, students at SCHOOL NAME may apply for supplemental education services such as tutoring. Parents interested in this option must choose a state-approved providers and a list is attached.

Please notify your principals in writing no later than DATE if you are interested in school transfer and/or supplemental education services during the YEAR school year. You will be contacted about the results of your request on or before DATE.

We want to continue serving your child and we will use all our available resources to help our students be successful. Building a high-quality school is a job for the school community and we need your support to reach that goal. Please contact NAME at CONTACT INFORMATION to provide us with input as we strive to help our students be successful. Thank you.

Sincerely,

Figure 5.3.   Sample Parent Letter

in mixed ways, including shock, surprise, and hostility. However, if the information has been communicated before, even if not exactly the same way, the reaction may be more sympathetic. The lesson to be learned here is take control of your communication early. A good way of doing that is to give the audience a general education about the NCLB law even before news about it appears. Be proactive and tell your story first. Always remain positive about the education opportunity the school is providing and the students you serve.

A tangible product is leading in the mind of a person attempting to market a school or the school district. In business a promotion campaign would be impossible without a product to promote or sell, such as a shirt, an appliance, or a food item. What possible products can we promote in education? The product of an educational organization can be the performance of students or programs and services. If you have high student achievement in the school, advertise it. If you have a comprehensive Advanced Placement program, advertise it. If you have small class sizes, advertise them. If you have national board certified teachers, advertise them. Reflect on your school. How do you meet the needs of the students, and what are the success indicators? Tell a success story, back it up with data, and promote your school. Effective communication is an important tool to provide information to customers and potential customers to remind them of the quality opportunities available in the schools. Effective communication is a critical tool to invite community support. Effective communication helps schools to pave the road to elevated student success and reach new heights in accountability.

CHAPTER REFLECTION

1. What are the similarities and differences between the Coleman research and the effective school research?
2. What is your top priority correlate for improving student achievement? Please explain why this is more important than the other effective school correlates.
3. You are presenting in a school faculty meeting. How do you explain the application of using school data to support the effective school correlates?
4. You are a school improvement consultant. Use a fishbone diagram to analyze the goal of creating a positive school climate.

5. You are preparing a school board presentation. What are the major strategies that you would use to let the school board know that the schools have not been making adequate yearly progress for one year? For three years?

REFERENCES

Coleman James Samuel. 1966. *Equality of Education Opportunity.* United States Department of Health, Education, and Welfare, Office of Education.

Demski, Dorreen. 2004. "Marketing Your Schools? Begin with a Solid Public Relations Program." *Wisconsin School News,* December.

Edmonds, R. R. 1979. "Effective Schools for the Urban Poor." *Educational Leadership* 37(2): 15–24.

Sargent, Judy K. 2003. *Data Retreat Workbook.* Green Bay, WI: Cooperative Educational Agency.

Conclusion

Many education reforms such as *A Nation at Risk* and Goals 2000 have come and gone, reinforcing the traditional wisdom that "this too shall pass." We can be confident that the effort of student improvement shall not pass if the core mission is student learning. The mission of learning prompted educators to answer the following three questions. What does it mean for each student to behave? How do we know when each student has behaved properly? How do we respond when students have challenges in behaving? The term "behavior" is used in the three questions because it has a broad implication to include learning as changed behavior.

Standards of behavior such as attendance, discipline, homework, and academic learning are the answers for the first question with connections to school policy and curriculum. The question "How do we know?" is answered by assessment with relevant data support. Decisions to adjust student behaviors or to modify a school program are based on data analysis and interpretation. What is the evidence that a student is not learning? A teacher is not effective? A school program is not serving the needs of students? The evidence can be addressed by information from a student record book, a teacher performance summary, a program survey, or other data-based reports.

We will never reach the destination of making successful students if we ask the right questions but fail to respond properly. Is the student or school improvement plan in alignment with our best education practices? Let the student data, the professional practice data, and the school community perception data drive the improvement goals.

Citizens expect educators to do their very best to improve schools and prepare students as productive citizens for tomorrow. This daunting task of improvement is achievable when the efforts are well coordinated and carefully thought out. Education is a life-shaping experience affecting the confidence and achievement of the learner. Helping every student to be 100-percent proficient and a successful learner is more than an enviable goal; it is a moral obligation.

REFERENCES

U.S. Department of Education. 1993. *Goals 2000 educate America: safe, disciplined, drug-free schools.* Washington D.C.

About the Authors

Ovid K. Wong is currently the dean of adult basic education with Triton College, River Grove, Illinois. He received his B.Sc. from the University of Alberta, his M.Ed. from the University of Washington, and his Ph.D. in curriculum and instruction from the University of Illinois. His experience in public education spans some twenty years from the classroom to the office of the assistant school superintendent. In 1989, Dr. Wong received the National Science Foundation's Outstanding Science Teacher in Illinois award and the Science Teaching Achievement Recognition (STAR) award by the National Science Teacher Association. In the same year he visited the former Soviet Union as the environmental science delegation leader with the student ambassador program. He was the first recipient of the outstanding alumni award by the University of Alberta in 1992 and also the first recipient of the distinguished alumni award by the College of Education at the University of Illinois in 1995. He is the author of twenty books and has received the Midwest Book Author award from the Children's Reading Roundtable of Chicago. His recent twelve books are dedicated to coaching teachers and students to effectively prepare for the state-mandated examination in Illinois, Michigan, and Ohio.

Ming-Long Lam is currently the manager of statistical research in SPSS, Inc., Chicago. He received his B.Sc. in mathematics and M.Phil. in statistics from the Chinese University of Hong Kong and his Ph.D.

in statistics from the University of Chicago. In addition to his technical research in statistical methodologies and algorithms, he constantly seeks to apply statistics to other disciplines. He recently coauthored with sociology researchers in a book chapter that studied return migration of Chinese in Toronto, Canada.